D1134568

Nurse on Call

Nurse on Call

Tales of a Blackcountry District Nurse

EDITH COTTERILL

CENTURY

LONDON   MELBOURNE   AUCKLAND   JOHANNESBURG

First published in 1986 by Century Hutchinson Ltd,
Brookmount House, 62–65 Chandos Place, Covent Garden,
London WC2N 4NW

Century Hutchinson Publishing Group (Australia) Pty Ltd,
16–22 Church Street, Hawthorn, Melbourne, Victoria 3122

Century Hutchinson Group (NZ) Ltd,
32–34 View Road, PO Box 40–086, Glenfield, Auckland 10

Century Hutchinson Group (SA) Pty Ltd,
PO Box 337, Bergvlei 2012, South Africa

Filmset in 11/12pt Linotron Sabon by
Deltatype Ltd., Ellesmere Port, Cheshire
Printed and bound in Great Britain by
Butler and Tanner Ltd, Frome, Somerset

British Library Cataloguing in Publication Data
Cotterill, Edith
Nurse on call: tales of a Blackcountry
district nurse.
1. Cotterill, Edith   2. Nurses —— England
—— Biography
I. Title
610.73'092'4   RT37.C6/

ISBN 0 7126 9521 4

Cover photograph by Trevor Leighton

— Contents —

CHAPTER ONE

— Refresher Course —

I WAS A district nurse of long standing. I have the feet to prove it, and for many years I plodded a Blackcountry beat. Patients can be a pleasure or a thorn in the flesh, but if you attend them long enough you become fond of them.

Mrs Tibbs was one of the thorns. She was a randy old warhorse squabbling with all and sundry and thriving on the belligerency but there was a bond between us which was a combination of affection and armed neutrality. Despite being very handicapped she lived alone, and if she had any relatives they had long since learned to keep their distance. When the Meals on Wheels service got into full swing it seemed just what she needed and I persuaded her to try it out.

The 'wheels' were represented by a converted van chauffered by a military-type retired gentleman and the 'meals' were produced by a brisk lady in green. Whenever I saw them they looked piping hot and delicious, but Mrs Tibbs yammered peevishly, 'I cor ate it', 'It's riffy!' or 'The taters aye dun'.

She speculated evilly on what went on between the military gent and the lady in green. 'The strumpet! An' 'es nowt but a bloody ponce!'

In vain I defended them, threatened her with slander or simply turned a deaf ear.

'No good tellin' yo nuthin',' she grieved. 'An' me a poor widder woman wi' me fittle 'arf cooked. No wonder me bally's all of a wamble.'

1

One day I arrived to be confronted with a pea on a saucer.

'Theer!' Mrs Tibbs indicated it triumphantly. 'I bet yo' cor ate that!'

Tentatively I squeezed the pea between thumb and forefinger and agreed; it was as hard as a bibble. But she was not to be put off with that.

'Goo on!' she bellucked. 'Yo try bitin' on it!'

Gingerly I bit hard on the offending pea which immediately shot across the room.

'Theer!' she rejoiced hugging herself. 'Yo cor ate it neither, an' what's more it's bin threw me once.'

* * *

When Dr Quinn arrived green from Ireland and with a brogue that could be cut with a knife, it caused much consternation amongst the patients he had inherited. 'The fule,' they chuntered. ''E cor even spake praper. 'E's bloody daft!'

He in turn suffered frustration. 'Oi'll niver understand them,' he mourned. 'They're for iver tellin' me they've not been to the ground. What in hell's name d'ya make o' that?'

Loyal to the locals, I expressed surprise that he, a medical man, did not recognize such a common term for constipation.

'Holy Mither o' God!' he keened. 'You're but another of 'em, an here's me thinkin' all nurses are Oirish!'

In an effort to make themselves better understood, patients bawled at the top of their voices; symptoms and sufferings were shouted aloud and the surgery waiting room became a place of entertainment. Hitherto secret ailments were disclosed to all and sundry. These were compensations indeed!

Mr Wagstaff was a patient of Dr Quinn's and Mr Wagstaff had pneumonia. He had got it specifically to annoy Mrs Wagstaff, for she resented having strangers traipsing about her immaculate house. In particular, she abhorred Dr Quinn, whose feet were very large and whose boots were always muddy. Poor man! He had no wife to clean them.

2

Nurses she regarded with suspicion as being no better than they should be. After all, when you thought of the things they did to folks! No self-respecting woman would be a nurse.

Mrs Wagstaff's mother and sister, replicas of herself, were part of the household and the three martinets darted about before me strewing newspapers where I might tread. 'Arter all,' reflected the old mother *sotto voce*, 'yo' doh know where 'ers bin!' Poor Mr Wagstaff. My heart went out to him.

In my earlier days pneumonia patients had a lysis and a crisis. They were propped up in Fowler's position and their labouring chests suffered the added burden of kaolin poultices. In recent years antibiotics have taken over, and a course of intramuscular injections, dexterously aimed at the tenderest part of the posterior, usually gets the sufferers on their feet in a week. (No doubt propelled there by their tortured buttocks!) Mr Wagstaff was the exception to the rule: he did not respond to treatment and his malaise dragged on. Neighbours talked darkly of the insurance policies with which he had been backed.

One morning my visit coincided with that of Dr Quinn. I groaned inwardly and edged for the door, but anticipating my escape, he took my arm and drew me outside onto the landing, followed by the relatives with ears cocked and eyes agog.

'Oi'll consult with nurse alone, please,' he said, and motioning me into the adjoining bathroom, closed the door on their frustrated faces.

Mrs Wagstaff's bathroom was as prim as herself and camouflaged with much candlewick. A prissy pink cover did its best to disguise the lavatory seat, and on this the young medico perched himself with a cigarette while I sat angled on the edge of the bath. Concern increased within me; however would I make up for lost time?

Having secured a captive audience, Dr Quinn waxed eloquent, oblivious to the fact that half the time I could not follow his jargon anyway. Outside, creaking floorboards reminded us of the waiting relatives. When his second cigarette had gone up in smoke, Dr Quinn finally prised himself off his perch on the pedestal and automatically, before I could stop him, pulled the dangling chain.

As the water flushed noisesomely we stared at each other in horror. Outside, a stony silence condemned us. There was only one way out – through the door. Sheepishly, we took it.

To the scandalized faces of the three women outside an explanation was futile, and if we had committed the most gross indecency we could not have looked more guilty.

Mr Wagstaff made a reluctant recovery and Dr Quinn left for pastures new, but whenever our paths crossed, the pursed lips of Mrs Wagstaff showed that she had not forgotten and, fool that I am, I blushed.

* * *

Miss Fallows' spacious Victorian house lay well back from the main road and was approached by means of a long overgrown driveway. The bell on the shabbily elegant front door did not respond, of course, but I found a back entrance and finally tracked down my new patient in a room which must once have been the kitchen. Obviously it was here she chose to live, and from the single bed in the corner, to sleep also. She was huddled in an old armchair by the fire and wore a cloche hat, a mangy fur coat and a pair of combinations. On her legs old lisle stockings adhered stickily to the ulcers which were my special problem.

I introduced myself and she received me graciously. Everyone, she said, had been so kind. A lady in green had been only a little while ago to clean her room and to cook her a meal. There had once, she reminisced, been many servants, with a nanny and later a governess for herself. She had been an only child, but after her parents died investments had gone wrong, money had evaporated. When the last family retainer had died also, she engaged a certain person to 'do for her' but the person had not been satisfactory and had persisted in bringing her unruly brood

4

of children with her. Now she was alone, except for a young woman who did her shopping. The price of food was scandalous, but she ate very little and it was obvious that she suffered from malnutrition. It was obvious, too, that she suffered from fleas.

Brittle black particles encrusted the tops of her stockings and when I cautiously turned them down, *pulex irritans* frolicked in abundance. Never had I seen so many fleas! Startled by the daylight, they leapt in all directions, particularly mine. Quickly I peeled off the stockings and threw them on the fire, but by now the fleas had invaded her combinations. As for the fur coat, I shuddered to think!

When I had prepared a basin of disinfectant and a bowl of hot water, I began the formidable task of cleaning Miss Fallows. She seemed surprisingly unperturbed. 'I suppose you get a lot of this,' she said. Fleas still cavorted (even cohabited!) undiminished, and I dropped them ruthlessly into the disinfectant. Poor things! They'd had such an idyllic existence until now, and they could not help being fleas. (I always did have a leaning towards Buddhism and the belief in the sanctity of life, however humble). It was obvious, however, that I was fighting a losing battle. I confessed to her that I would have to report the fleas to the authorities; they were too prolific for me to deal with and I must protect the other patients. She did not protest. Worse was to come.

When I came to remove the cloche hat it was stuck fast. I prised it off and found why: her hair was cemented solid with nits and excreta of multitudinous *pediculus capitis* ('bogies' to the layman). The only thing was to clip her hair close to the scalp. She was unhappy about this, but consented. It came off hard and solid like a space helmet and I tossed it on the fire where it spat and crackled furiously. 'Sorry, Buddha!' I would have to bring delousing lotion tomorrow; meanwhile I put the cloche back on. It would keep her warm.

With Miss Fallows' permission I went upstairs in search of clean clothes. She herself had not been up for years, and there, shades of Arthur Negus, was a Victorian paradise.

Surely under that thick coating of dust was Chippendale? Under that grime Sèvres porcelain? In the wardrobes I found garments that could have graced the Victoria and Albert Museum; in the drawers hand-embroidered underwear, yellow with age. Rich tapestries hung, rotten to the touch, a world of treasures long abandoned. Fascinated I wandered into what must have been a boxroom. An aloof rocking horse and grimy, wax-faced dolls stared back at me. An old stamp album opened at random displayed a Penny Black. In a corner, excellent pewter and lustreware lay cluttered together, and the bright blue and orange of old Staffordshire china defied the dust.

Recalling my duties I hurried back to a bedroom, collected a few of the most suitable garments and returned below stairs. While dressing Miss Fallows, I told her of the treasure trove that I suspected she had and warned her to let no unauthorized person have access to it. She was far from senile. If things were arranged properly she could afford to spend the rest of her life in comfort.

By the time I left, I was in no little discomfort. Sternly I told myself it was psychological, but when slowing down in heavy traffic, I caught a glimpse of black specks playing hop-scotch on my legs. I found it difficult to concentrate on my driving and got several V signs from lorry drivers. Purposefully I made for home. Once there I ran the bath, added disinfectant and got in with my clothes on. When I set off again in fresh uniform I was alarmingly late, but I had taken the precaution of notifying the establishment and extracting from them a promise for immediate action.

When I reached Mrs Tibbs, she was vigorously wielding a wooden back-scratcher. Outside in the yard, her home help was shaking her bloomers. We compared notes; she was revealed as Miss Fallows' 'lady in green'.

I finally arrived home with an ominous crawling sensation on the back of my neck and my husband's investigation found several great grey grandfather bogies (or were they grandmothers and still productive?). Head lice have chameleon qualities and change colour to blend with the hair of their host, but obviously these had not had time to adapt (or else the cares of the day had added to the grey hairs I already lamented!). My husband made a further painstaking and lucrative search of my head and then we anointed ourselves with bogey deterrent. It had to stay on for twenty-four hours, and tomorrow his workmates, the children's schoolmates and my patients would recognize the obnoxious effluvia. It was not the first time, and they would all keep their distance.

That night I was disturbed by an unusual hump under the bedclothes. It was my husband anxiously searching his person with a torch. We spent the rest of the night flea hunting. I bet Buddha never had fleas! By morning he had lost himself a convert.

The children went to school bearing flea bites on their necks, and at nine o'clock promptly and in a truculent mood, I phoned the establishment. The condescending young man who answered said he himself had visited the lady in question, had found nothing amiss and on examining her bed, the obvious source of contamination, had found it to be unblemished. I must, he said, be collecting the parasites elsewhere and his tone suggested that I might be breeding them myself. Adroitly, before I could retaliate, he rang off. Furiously I leapt into the car and drove like Jehu to his department.

Poor chap! I obviously shocked his sensitivity by confronting him so precipitously in the flesh, and what flesh! I am one of those unfortunates who blossom forth in weals and bumps at the bite of a flea, and my hair hung lank, greasy and odoriferous. Vehemently I demanded he should accompany me to Miss Fallows and with bad grace he did so. He watched while I dressed her legs and of evidence there was plenty; in fact the creatures appeared to have propagated overnight. Then he kindly suggested to her that she should be admitted to a geriatric ward for a few days while her room was fumigated. In front of her I mentioned the relics above stairs and asked that her interests should be safeguarded. This appeared to be right up his street and he

7

thawed visibly. He had, he said, a considerable knowledge of antiques.

While they were debating, I made a cursory search of the bed. He was right there; none of the telltale marks which always denote the presence of fleas! It was quite incredible. We discussed it on the way back, but were unable to solve the enigma and parted amicably. I noted with satisfaction that he was surreptitiously scratching under his armpit.

The following evening I called to see Miss Fallows in the geriatric ward where she had been installed. She had, I felt, had a raw deal which she had accepted graciously and when she came out of hospital she would again be my responsibility. She sat propped up in bed wearing a capeline bandage on her head and was delighted to see me. I had taken her a boudoir cap, a Christmas gift of several years past, frilled and beribboned and definitely not me. On Miss Fallows it gave her an air of aristocracy. Everyone, she said, had been so kind; there was the possibility her house might be bought and converted into flats, with herself on the ground floor, or else in a small council flat.

She was exhilarated by the prospect of financial improvement and by the interest which had been taken in her. 'But it does seem strange', she said, 'sleeping here. I've always spent the night in my old chair, dear. Better for my chest, you know. Haven't slept in a bed for years!'

*　　*　　*

I had done my SRN training before the war, but when I got married and had a family I looked forward to time to myself. I should have known better. In 1952 for the first time we had a full complement of nurses on the district and belatedly the powers that be decided that some of us were a bit long in the tooth. It was many years since we had taken our training, so refresher courses were being organized to bring us up-to-date. We none of us wanted to go but it was not optional, and I was chosen as the first victim. I made vain protests and bleated feebly about having to leave my family. (They, ungrateful wretches, were delighted and began planning all they would do in my absence.)

Brochures arrived and a railway permit from Birmingham to London finalized the arrangements. I was instructed to take a set of uniform as the course would include one hospital visit. I was horrified, having taken it for granted that uniform would be worn throughout the course. If it was to be worn only once, what would I wear the rest of the time? I practically lived in uniform, and certainly nothing in my meagre wardrobe was adequate for the Great Metropolis.

I hate buying new clothes but on my day off I planned a shopping expedition. Threatened by my family not to come back with navy blue, for which I have an affinity, I settled for a little grey suit which buttoned up to a round collarless neck. It was crying out for a white blouse with a Peter Pan collar and I found the very thing in the girls' department. It wasn't very accommodating, leaving me with a bare midriff, and it wouldn't button over the bust, but the neck line was perfect and nothing else would show under the jacket. I bought two; they were just what my younger daughter needed to supplement her school uniform and I wouldn't be wearing them after the course.

I returned home pleased with my purchases.

For days preceding my departure I rushed round like one demented, laying in food stocks as if for a seige, cleaning, washing and pinning notices on doors:

'Have you turned the hot water off?'
'Have you left the gas on?'
'Have you fed the fish?'
'Have you walked the dog?'
'Please water the plants.'
'Have the animals been fed?'
'Is the cat shut in a bedroom?'
'Go back and have another look.'
'Stop – have you got your key?'

At last the time came to go. The family saw me off at Birmingham and gave me alarming lists from which to choose their 'coming home' presents. Anything, they assured me, was available in London. I felt apprehensive on the journey and kept remembering things I had hitherto forgotten. I wondered if they would find the chip-pan which I had hidden under a bed. If they did, they would surely set themselves on fire before my return.

My new quarters were near Marble Arch, but I have no bump of location so following my husband's instructions, and feeling very extravagant, I took a taxi. On arrival I was shown to my room which was small and spartan, with a chair, a tallboy and a narrow bed. I was thankful to have it to myself. There was just time to change before the supper gong, when district nurses of all shapes and sizes swarmed into the dining room. Most were soberly garbed; those who were not stuck out like sore fingers, and I viewed my grey suit and fresh white collar with smug satisfaction. During the meal we all eyed each other suspiciously and ate in silence, except for a few who recognized each other as past acquaintances and were acclaimed with cries of joy. There was a sprinkling of male nurses, but I had never worked with a male nurse then, and took a dim view of them.

We dined off rather stringy cold ham and limp salad, with custard tart and prunes for afters. When we filed out again we were each handed a round disc, backed with a pin, on which to inscribe our names for identification purposes. Foolishly I wrote on mine, 'I like Ike', and deservedly became mistaken for I. Likle, degenerating as we became more familiar to Likle Tot (I'm a long five foot seven!).

The girls – we were all girls again – who occupied the rooms adjoining mine ganged up with me and, unbidden, came in. Cameron was a dark, dour Scot, but Shingles (and immediately dubbed Herpes Zoster) was plump and bouncy with beautiful hair the colour of ripe manure. Disastrously, she always wore pink. We sat talking shop until midnight when the lights were automatically switched off and we were left to grope our way to bed in the dark. The radiator at the head of my bed gurgled and belched all night. I put my pillow at the foot of the bed and lay the wrong way round, but the rest of the night was sleepless. A gong sounded at 6.30 a.m. and at 7 a.m. an unseen call-girl thundered on all the doors announcing breakfast at 7.30 a.m.

The tables were laid with small packets of cereal and large packets of All-Bran, and we lined up at the self-service for the second course, which was an egg on a slither of pork luncheon meat.

The first lecture at nine o'clock was committed to introducing the syllabus and was given by the formidable sister-tutor who was in charge of us, and who promptly reduced us to the status of junior probationers. Her name was Miss Collins and so, naturally, to us she became Lottie. She adjured us to make the most of this wonderful opportunity of learning, and not to waste the taxpayers' money.

The days dragged on; meals followed the same pattern, figs sometimes supplanting the prunes, to the discomfort of denture wearers. Most of the lectures were old-hat; those on new drugs were our greatest need, but names were complicated, defying spelling and pronunciation, and our no-longer-youthful brains found difficulty in assimilating and retaining knowledge. Frantically we scribbled notes in exercise-books in deference to the taxpayers and numbed our earnest bottoms on the slatted seats.

District work involves the heavy lifting of helpless patients. Most of us had been doing this for years in our own peculiar ways with no ill-effects; now we were told we had been doing it all wrong and at great risk to ourselves. We were taught anew how to lift in pairs. (No use protesting that we all travelled alone and must needs manage unaided. Lottie withered us with a glance.) Awkwardly we obeyed instructions, heaving each other around in alien and most inelegant postures. Several nurses who had been hoisting heavy patients uneventfully for twenty years or more pulled muscles, or worse, and hobbled round for the remainder of the course in a crouched position, walking as if with two left legs and with an agonized expression.

Eminent lecturers honoured us, sometimes starting as late

as nine o'clock at night in order to fit us in with their busy schedules. There was no free time for shopping or having a meal out, and after supper long queues formed at the phone in the corridor to enquire anxiously about young families left at home.

It was after 10.30 p.m. one night before I achieved my first call home. My younger daughter answered and un-diplomatically I demanded to know why she was still up. She replied indignantly that they were busy decorating (Heavens!) and where was the chip-pan? When I asked for father, he was in the bath, having covered himself in paint; my elder daughter was out with a new boyfriend (instantly rape was uppermost in my mind!); everything else was fine, except the cat was missing and Bo'sun, my old whippet, was pining and refusing food. Oh, and Grandad had hit his head with the chopper. What on earth were they thinking of, letting Grandad loose with a chopper? At this point, and to further demands as to the whereabouts of the chip-pan, we were cut off. It was all very disturbing. I wished I hadn't phoned and lay awake all night worrying about them.

Entertainment had been arranged in the form of a visit to the ballet and a trip to see the Ceremony of the Keys. The latter, climactic as the chimes of ten reverberated, was most stirring, and the sombre sight of Traitors' Gate alone set me back several centuries. Of the ballet I was not sure, but I was inspired to caricature the male dancer on a postcard for the family and to inscribe it:

> Ballet man so lithe and light,
> Leaping high with all your might,
> Pirouetting in delight,
> Aren't your drawers a trifle tight?
> Don't you think that maybe you
> Could wear a little tutu too?

One day was spent visiting a modern mental establish-ment, but there was nothing institutional about it, for none of the staff wore uniform and the patients wandered about at will. We were divided into individual groups, each of which was provided with an escort. Ours was an immaculate young man; his suit was Saville Row and his linen exquisite. His hands fascinated me, being beautifully shaped and manicured, and he was a delightful escort who charmed us all. The decor and furnishings of the establishment were sumptuous, with costly curtains and lush fitted carpets. As our companion said, patients who chose to live in such luxury instead of working for their bread were not so daft after all. We, he insinuated, but with forgiving grace, were the 'softies'.

Occasionally we met up with the other groups for discussion. The patients were allowed to join in; one moon-faced woman with haywire hair came to us each in turn and we spoke soothingly to her, anxious to show compassion. At mid-morning we were given coffee and biscuits in the dining room, where a glamorous female introduced herself as night sister. She explained her many duties, questioned us expertly on ours, and was very interested and most deferential. Altogether we had a very enjoyable day with an excellent lunch and tea, and then Lottie put in an appearance to round off the day and thank matron for her hospitality.

The moon-faced woman came forward and said it had been a pleasure, and we realized with horror that she was the matron. We felt even more foolish when we found out later that 'night sister' was 'Pretty Poll, the persistent prostitute', and that our charming escort was a rapist of the worst order. On the way back, when one of our group found her purse was missing with all her cash and return permit, we deemed it wiser to keep quiet and have a whip round for her amongst ourselves.

The refresher course was due to finish on Saturday at 12.30 p.m., the forenoon being occupied with a rounding-off session with Lottie. There was a general panic to inquire about trains when someone remembered that London shops are closed on Saturday afternoons. No last minute chance of a shopping spree! I decided to get the first possible train, but not to forewarn the folk back home; then I could get their presents en route in Birmingham and perhaps pass them off as London-bought.

On Friday night, for the first time, we were free at 7.30 p.m. and Cameron and Herpes planned a trip into the wicked city. Herpes had always wanted to visit Dirty Dick's, so we enlisted a taxi and left the rest to the driver. Dick's certainly was dirty! It harboured a motley crew: sailors, bearded Bohemians, elegant ladies and foreign visitors all jostled together. We managed to establish ourselves in a dusty corner draped with cobwebs and Herpes, being the most knowledgeable, volunteered to fetch the drinks.

Now I have nothing against drinking at the right time and place, but I have only to imbibe so much as one intoxicating potion and my nose bleeds fiercely the next day. I hastily explained this foible to Herpes and asked her to get me a soft drink that at least looked as though it might be something more interesting. She was away some time, and I don't know what she brought me, as she said one of the sailors propping up the bar had advised her. Anyway it was jolly nice, though surprisingly costly.

The place livened up after a bit and we became quite giggly and skittish. We bought three rounds between us and Herpes obligingly fetched them all. I stuck to my original drink to play safe, but after the third I passed out. Somehow they got me back in a taxi and, with the co-operation of our contemporaries, into my bed.

I woke the next morning with a thundering headache and a mouth like the bottom of a birdcage. Cameron and Herpes came in to view me, and after a conference decided I could miss breakfast, but must attend Lottie's last lecture, as it involved signing the register to ensure no one had escaped early. I struggled into my clothes while they were at breakfast and made an attempt to pack my case, but red-hot fingers of pain probed every crevice of my skull and several times I was violently sick. Cameron and Herpes helped me down to the lecture room and everyone made room for us to install ourselves on the back row, away from Lottie's eagle eye.

Lottie's lecture was a brief resumé of all that had gone before, dwelling finally on the problem of lifting which we had so lamentably failed to solve. She called up two of the male nurses to demonstrate – their muscles were less vulnerable – and asked for a volunteer to be the patient. There were no offers.

'Come along,' she cried. 'You at the end of the back row, don't sit skulking there!' There was still no response. Herpes nudged me and dazedly I realized I was the one at the end of the back row. Painfully, with throbbing head, I stumbled forward and up the steps on to the platform. Lottie beckoned me into the chair which stood between the two stalwart male nurses.

'Come,' she cried, warming to her subject, 'off with your coat!' Briskly she had my grey jacket unbuttoned and off before I remembered the little white blouse gaping beneath. Futilely I tried to pull it together to hide the expanse of bra and bare midriff now exposed to all and sundry. There was a rending sound from under the armpits; miserably I gave up and sat bog-eyed and blotto, shamed before them all.

My disgrace was complete; nothing worse could happen to me now.

But it could.

And it did.

Slowly, insidiously, relentlessly, my nose began to bleed.

*   *   *

The refresher course had not done much to improve my ego. It only made me realize what an ignoramous I was. Uneasy at heart I cadged a Mims list from the chemist to compare with the notes I had scribbled during the lectures on drugs and began taking Honnor Morton's dictionary to bed with me. Faced with such opposition my husband retired with the sulks and a hot-water bottle.

I raked out my old lecture notes and when I opened them it was like a trip into the Dark Ages.

15

Afterwards I lay staring into the darkness, reviewing, like the proverbial drowning man, all the events in my life which had brought me to this pass.

CHAPTER TWO

— Dropped by the Zeppelins —

LIFE BEGAN FOR me in 1916 in the dark dank cellar of our house when Mother took refuge from the Zeppelin raids which devastated the Blackcountry, then a great hive of industry. Father, ever resourceful, installed a makeshift bed, a light and a gas fire but nonetheless it was a cellar and the month was January.

According to newspapers of that period the Zeppelins, like monstrous fish in the sky, flew so low that men, having no other weapons, threw stones at them in futile retaliation.

Such singular conditions in parturition caused my Mother to lose her milk and my sister Hilda queued long hours to provide my sustenance, but she had been an only child and the joy of having a sister compensated for this. I was an evil child and Mother told me that I had been dropped by the Zeppelins. I was proud of the distinction; it was one up on my friend Cecil who had been dropped by a stork. Cecil's mother and mine went shopping together, sharing problems and the articles in their women's magazines which were then becoming so popular. Cecil and I followed hand in hand behind them listening avidly to what the magazines advised, for the most debated topic was how to bring up children and we knew that we would be on the receiving end. One of the scourges of civilization, they declared, was constipation, but if children were trained from an early age to perform every day at a given time, preferably after breakfast, it would establish a desirable habit.

17

Cecil and I rolled our eyes at each other on hearing this, and sure enough before long we were incarcerated each morning in our respective WCs and told 'to go' regardless of our inclinations. I've often wondered since how many prolapsed rectums were the result of this system. Mother would stand outside the door, in itself very offputting, asking anxiously, 'Avez-vous fini?' (Hilda had just begun to learn French), and if I hadn't, I was a naughty, obstinate child. I soon learned to tear up the squares of newspaper which hung on the back of the lavatory door and pull the chain quickly before she could investigate.

Cecil suffered likewise, as did many other children, for now the magazines began to print remedies to promote evacuation and our mothers' shopping lists included licorice powder, turkey rhubarb, Black Jack, Gregory's powder and the ingredients for brimstone and treacle. Turkey rhubarb came in two varieties: a dark brown paste which could be rolled into pills, and a root resembling rough hewn wood. Mother favoured the latter and kept a chunk in the machine drawer, handy to carve off a lump for me to swallow when the mood took her. I felt its rough passage all the way down to my stomach and was then two-double for the rest of the day.

Cecil was a solicitous child. My shoes were always bought a size too large so that I would grow into them, consequently I suffered from blisters on my heels. Cecil would squeeze my hand and say, 'Never mind. When we grow up I shall marry you and buy some ointment for your poor feet.' Our happy relationship lasted until we were four years old and went to different schools, but we still met during vacations to condole with each other on the eccentricities of mothers and to help carry their shopping home.

One evening Mother and I called to find that poor Cecil was ill with stomach pains.

'You know what's wrong with him, don't you?' cried his anxious parent. 'He hasn't been to the ground for two

18

whole days! I've tried everything, but he's still not had a passage through him.' She was preparing some evil concoction.

'If this doesn't shift him, nothing will.'

Despite pitiful pleading poor Cecil was forced to take it. 'Hold his nose!' someone cried, but his distress was too great to be borne and I rushed to his rescue, punching and kicking and screaming 'Let him be!' But I was bundled from the room and the last sight I had of my little friend was his anguished face as hands restrained him, held his nose and forced him to swallow the lethal brew which was to perforate his appendix.

After my outburst – and in someone else's house! – I was sent to bed and ostracized by my family, but I learned from other children that Cecil had been taken to hospital for an operation. A few days later, en route for school, I heard two women talking and Cecil's name was mentioned. '. . . bosted appendix. After 'is operation 'e wus in such pain 'e tore' the bandages off!' 'They atta tie 'is 'onds ter the rails at the top of 'is bed.' 'Poor little bugger 'es better off jed.'

Horror seized me. I ran and hid under the canal bridge where I could weep unseen and swear a lifelong vendetta against doctors and nurses who had so abused him, and I was filled with a great bitterness that I, his best friend, should not have been told of his death. When I was sufficiently recovered to make my way to school, I was very late and had to stand in a corner for the rest of the morning with my hands on my head. My arms ached unbearably but it gave me some comfort to think I was, in some small way, sharing his sufferings.

*   *   *

After Cecil I tended to avoid other children and spent hours on the splendid swing which Father had erected for us in the garden. It was a very large garden, and when Dad was digging Mother sent me to follow in his wake with an empty tin in which to collect worms for the white leghorn hens of which she was inordinately proud. When I was very young I felt sorry for the poor chickens having to eat raw worms and so I cooked them on the garden fire, stirring them with a stick until they were well done. When I was old enough to realize the cruelty of my act, I was so overcome with remorse that I have ever since been trying to vindicate myself by extricating worms from the ridiculous situations into which they get themselves, and always after heavy rain I can be seen gathering the squirming creatures off the roads and paths where they get trodden underfoot to dump them in the nearest gardens. They're not easy to pick up and passers-by, walking round me, eye each other significantly, while my whippets standing patiently by until I am done have exactly the same expressions on their aristocratic faces.

Father was proud of his garden but Bina, our next door neighbour, harboured innumerable cats and three goats called Jacket, Wescut and Trousers. Their own plot had long since been reduced to a barren tract, trodden hard and smooth and devoid of anything edible, so the cats came over to scratch up our soil and do whatever it is cats have to do, and the nights were rent with the caterwauling of feline miscegenations. What a mercy such clamorous manifestations of concupiscence are confined to cats! Meanwhile the goats with lascivious eyes peered through the fence, coveting our verdant pasturage and, for want of something better, surreptitiously nibbled the fence.

Bina was a large lovable lady. Her clothes always looked as though they had been just thrown on so that she gave the impression of a vast unmade bed. As well as the cats and the goats she had a lodger who was writing another Bible and believed he was the new Messiah. Both the lodger and the goats had long silky beards but whereas the lodger, with his domed forehead and lean sad face, really did have a look of Jesus Christ, the goats with their horns and wicked yellow eyes were personifications of the Devil. One day, driven to a state of dementia by their frustration, they demolished the

20

fence, rampaging through like an invading horde to plunder Father's cabbage patch.

The lodger, taking advantage of the breech they had created, followed and came unbidden into the kitchen where I was deep in a pictorial history book, for Hilda and I were weaned on history and Father reckoned that even children's books should be informative. The lodger took me on his knee and fondled me with long slender fingers. I had just reached Boadicea and the illustration depicted her riding post haste through the enemy ranks in her war chariot; great mutilating scythes projected from the axles of the wheels and decapitated heads all wearing expressions of extreme astonishment were hurtling in every direction.

'Thats me! That's me!' cried the lodger, pointing to the various heads, and to be honest they weren't unlike him. What a kind man, I thought, and very affectionate. Diplomatically I diverted his attention to other periods of history, explaining all the pictures as Father had told them to me. There was Alfred the Great daydreaming in a cloud of smoke fit to choke him but oblivious of the cakes smouldering on the hearth, Robert Bruce mesmerized by a very obscene spider, and Joan of Arc clad only in her shimmy on top of a bonfire holding up imploring arms to a gaggle of angels on a cloud just out of reach.

The kitchen door was ajar and there seemed to be an altercation going on outside. I could hear Mother's agitated voice and Bina's hoarse whisper pleading to 'let him be until they arrived'. Meanwhile the lodger had become very maudlin over poor Joan; he pressed his lips to her picture with exaggerated fervour. 'That's you! That's you!' he cried, transferring his kisses to me, and hastily I turned over the page. It was a great mistake, for the next picture was one of Columbus in a very unlikely boat about to set sail on his discovery of America. He should have been horsewhipped for finding it, cried my friend, for America was a den of iniquity which would eventually bring about the end of the world. An even greater disaster awaited us on the next page, for there were the Pilgrim Fathers in their broad white

21

collars and tall black hats as they disembarked from the *Mayflower* and landed on Plymouth Rock. Better by far cried the lodger had Plymouth Rock landed on the Pilgrim Fathers! He was really roused and I was wondering what next when there was a scuffle and uniformed men rushed in carrying a peculiar back-to-front jacket with long tapering sleeves. They had it on him in a trice and trussed him like a chicken. I bunted them but it was of no avail: he was rostled into a black van and I was sent to bed. There was no justice for little children and new prophets.

*　　*　　*

When one is small one notices things near to the ground. We had an old sofa in the kitchen under which everyone stuffed their shoes, and there was just enough room for me too if turkey rhubarb or bedtime were imminent. Next to the sofa, at floor level, was a small cupboard in which lived a little tabby cat with white paws. She was called Spats and I loved her dearly. Whenever Mother saw her at large she would cry, 'In that cupboard!' and the little creature would dash to open the door and get inside quick, then a tiny white paw would emerge and pull the door to. There she lived and had her being and took refuge from Bina's belligerent felines. It was customary to give cats only bread and milk to encourage them to supplement their diet with mice but I saved many a titbit for Spats, risking Mother's ire, for she had once read that our kidneys were embedded in fat and she firmly believed that it was necessary to consume large quantities to keep them in position. She was always threatening us with 'floating kidneys' if we didn't eat our quota of fat, but I had learned by sleight of hand to transfer mine to my knicker leg and later to Spats's cupboard. Father, for his part, adjured us to chew our food forty-three times and never hold our water.

Although Mother enjoyed shopping with her friend, the bulk of our provisions came from one of Grandfather's shops in Dudley-Port. It was an accepted fact that all the family should patronize it, but what a chore when you lived a distance away as we did! There were no buses, of course, so once a week Hilda and I, armed with commodious shopping bags and a long shopping list (for one must never be accused of cheese paring), set off by the quickest route which was along the canal.

Hilda was the most important person in my life; to be with her, to have her to myself for that considerable time, was a joy. I longed to be like her with her striking blue eyes and blonde pigtails, but however I tried to emulate her I still remained the 'enfant terrible'. She was being groomed for teachership and Dad's pride in her was great; it had been his dearest wish to become a teacher but his father, a local farmer, had need of his sons to work the land and took him from school at the age of twelve. He never forgave Grandad and got his own back by getting himself a job at the gasworks. As we plodded along the towpath where strong patient horses dragged heavy barges of coal, Hilda would instruct me in little French songs such as 'Frère Jacques' and 'Quand trois poulets' and on the local flora such as ragged-Robin, Bird's-foot trefoil and toadflax which, despite the environment, was abundant. Surreptitiously I lagged behind munching the sweet milky buds of the pignuts and popping some into the little muff which hung on a cord round my neck and into which I could stuff my hands on the outward journey. Better not let Hilda see, for Mother always questioned her as to my behaviour and though she wasn't a telltale she was inordinately conscientious. If Mom knew about the pignuts she would immediately visualize their contamination by dogs or boatmen – or what about all those horses? Horses had 'Bots!' – and she would dose me with one of her terrible concoctions guaranteed to rostle undesirable contents from a child's stomach in one agonizing motion.

After leaving the canal we had quite a trek by road before reaching the shop where our great aunts Polly and Zilla served, scooping sugar from large sacks into strong dark-blue paper bags. Everything was scrupulously weighed and before we left, heavy laden, Aunt Polly would deftly convert

two squares of papers into cone-shaped bags which Aunt
Zilla would fill with licorice sweets for us. Ugh! I looked
longingly at the jars of sherbet and gobstoppers but, alas,
those were not for us. What a trudge was the homeward
journey hampered with our heavy bags while only five
minutes from home was Owen Street, then an excellent
shopping centre with a street market every Tuesday and
everything so much cheaper.

One bleak day as we prepared for our weekly jaunt and
the wind howled outside like a beast waiting to attack us,
Hilda cried, 'This is ridiculous! It's the last time we shall go!'
Mother and I gaped at her flabbergasted. Mom was
buttoning up my gaiters, brown leather ones which were
slipped on over my shoes and secured under the instep by a
piece of elastic; they came to just above the knee and were
buttoned up the sides with small round buttons which
needed careful manipulation with a hook. She paused,
button-hook in hand, for secretly she had long hankered
after the fleshpots of Owen Street. After a moment's
speculation she said, 'Then you must tell them. I'm only an
in-law.' What were 'in-laws' I wondered, and if she was one
why were not we?

It was a silent trip this time as Hilda strode purposefully
ahead rehearsing what she should say; she certainly
wouldn't back out for what she said was always gospel
truth. How brave she was to defy the family. When we had
been served but before the ritual of the sweets she spoke:
'Thank you Aunt Polly, thank you Aunt Zilla, you have
always been so kind to us but I'm afraid we shall not be
coming again. I'm sure you will understand it is such a long
way to carry provisions.'

Aunt Polly went red and Aunt Zilla went white, but they
both were struck dumb and we escaped before they
recovered. What a wonderful sister I had! There was
nothing she could not do if she had a mind to.

A few years later when she left home to teach at a
boarding school at Broadstairs I was stunned, for I never
believed that such a thing could happen. But that night as I

lay in the big bed which we two had shared the whole of my life and I put out a hand to touch the cold spot where she should have been, then I believed and I knew nothing would ever be the same again. And it never was.

*　　*　　*

Sometimes in the dark hours of the night I woke to hear strange happenings in the street outside and bright lights trailed across the ceiling, bathing the whole room in an unearthly glow. Curiosity overcame fear as I crept to the window to watch a cavalcade of jingling carts pass by; shadows of men and horses thrown by the swinging lanterns loomed sinister and fearsome and elongated out of all proportion. When I crept, chill and trembling, back to bed it was to dream of smugglers with 'brandy for the parson and baccy for the clerk'.

Actually they were 'night soil men', and the cargo in those carts was nothing more than the unwholesome fruit of the town's privies which was liable to be dumped on any open ground, especially where there was an accommodating hollow, so that great pools of excreta scarred the district. From time to time some inebriate, heading for home across the fields, would stumble into the mire and the night would be rent with frantic cries, ''Elp! 'elp! I'm in the shit!' Then men, all dummicked with sleep, would fumble for their trousers and there would be the clatter and hoarse cries of rescuers as they hurried with ropes and planks to drag out the victim, now probably up to his neck in the bog.

We had a privy at the bottom of our garden next to the ash pit, for there were no bins. Inside the privy was a bench seat with three holes, one large, one medium and one small, all very social, but we didn't use it for Father, very go-ahead, had installed a water closet at the end of the veranda with a large WC painted on the door. Complete strangers came for miles just to pull the chain and marvel at the wonder of it all. Father was proud of his loo and spent long periods there with the morning paper, much to the annoyance of Mother when she was pipped at the pedestal. Ironically the un-

25

dulating field at the bottom of our garden had been commandeered by the night soil men. Father was furious and wrote protestations to the council every time the wind blew in our direction.

Once as a small child I had clawed my way through our hedge to explore the field. It was a day of green and gold and bumble bees and heaven-high a tiny speck that was a lark trilled joyfully. A little way ahead grew a young hawthorn tree – 'bread and cheese' we called them and ate their tenderest leaves, but this one was curiously foreshortened, its branches low to the ground – and at my feet spread a great brown expanse, the crusted surface smooth and crying out to be run across. I ran and was engulfed in excrement; giant suckers tugged at my feet and my fingers clutched at nothingness. The more I struggled the deeper I sank; I threshed about abortively then suddenly touched something solid, staunch, immovable to which I clung; it was the hawthorn tree. No wonder it looked out of proportion: two-thirds of its trunk was submerged in mire. I clawed upwards until I could reach the lowest branch and was able to drag myself out. As I lay on the bank exuding filth, only the skylark was witness to my plight and I was already planning how to escape detection.

A brook ran at the bottom of the field and I lay in it sullying its clear water with my abomination until, despite the heat of the day, a chill penetrated my bones and then I made my way, bedraggled and unwholesome, homewards.

'Wherever have you been?' cried my poor Mother.

'In the brook,' I truthfully replied and was speedily dunked in the large brown earthenware sink which was conveniently full of hot soapy suds and scrubbed with pink carbolic.

When Dad came home Mother said, 'Our Edie's fallen in the brook. Just you smell her. You know what that is, if it's seeping in the brook there's no knowing where it will be carried, into the drinking water I shouldn't wonder.'

Solemnly and without preamble Father reached for his writing pad.

*   *   *

Night soil was also carried in barges on the canal to defile
the outlying countryside. Bill Perry the Tipton Slasher, for
years Boxing Champion of all England, worked on one of
these conveyances as a child and this intrepid pugilist, one-
time darling of the aristocracy, when his career was finished
was reduced to his former job and again became a Tipton
'night sile mon'.

Tipton, my home town, was known as the 'Venice of the
Midlands', not because of its arts and crafts and antiquity
but because it was interspersed with a multitude of canals.
These provided cheap transport for coal and heavy goods;
in fact brickyards, coal yards and factories were purposely
built near to them and made more accessible by long arms
from the canals which penetrated to their very heart.

There was a constant toing and froing of great horse-
drawn barges as silently and at very little cost they did the
jobs now taken over by the monstrous juggernauts. The
boatmen were a race apart and brought up their families in
little cabins built on the boat. Boxing was a popular sport;
men fought barefisted, sometimes to the death, for a mere
pittance or maybe just a provocation.

There was the constant sound of industry both day and
night and the Aurora Borealis had nothing on us, for the
night skies were illuminated by the blast furnaces. It is said
that when travelling by rail through the Blackcountry
Queen Victoria always insisted on having the blinds drawn
because she couldn't bear to see it. No credit to her, for it
was the heartbeat of her domain.

The local works had 'bulls' which emitted a loud hollow
sound at given times to apprehend their workers of the
hour. Each works 'bull' varied so that it was easy to
discriminate between them. I had a great fear of being late
for school as reprisals were vicious; if Mother hadn't got rid
of me before the nine o'clock bull went there was the devil to
pay. Here Uncle Walter would invariably come to the
rescue, for he delivered our milk from the family dairy at

about this time. He was a fine handsome fellow and ignoring my squawls he would dump me in his float and set off at a spanking pace to get me there on time. As I stood in front of him between the reins with the wind in my hair and the horse going clipperty-clop, its brasses all ajingle, I thought I was Boadicea in her chariot and was the envy of all my schoolmates.

*   *   *

It was a dark and dreadful Monday for Tipton on 6 March 1922, when there was an explosion in a factory not far from home. A group of girls had been dismantling ammunition, a job they had been doing for several weeks and for which they were paid one shilling and sixpence (approximately 7½p) per hundredweight of gunpowder, which they extracted from cartridges and put into boxes. In the room where they worked blazed an open fire and the holocaust created when fire and gunpowder eventually made contact beggars description.

After the conflagration there were the hoarse cries of men running and women with shawls on their heads and tears on their faces. One girl escaped, none were killed, but the victims, bereft of hair and clothing, ran about stark naked, their poor flesh consumed beyond repair and their blackened and mutilated faces unidentifiable even to their parents. When they could be caught they were wrapped in sacks, a pile of which was lying nearby, and placed on available vehicles which had been commandeered; cars were few and far between.

As the grisly procession made its two-mile journey to the hospital their fearful cries and pitiful pleas for water were heartrending. By midnight twelve were dead and within a few hours seven more had also died.

Our vicar, who had been very unpopular for his puritanical fervour, gavé all the skin that could be taken from him for those who lingered on; even these days skin grafting is a precarious business, so I'm afraid it didn't do much for the girls but it did a power of good for the vicar.

28

As I write I can see through my window the plinth which marks their common grave. Hannah, the oldest of the group, was sixteen years of age, the rest were fourteen and fifteen, except little Lizzie and Priscilla who were both thirteen, and sometimes in the quiet hours I imagine I hear 'the laughter of little girls playing at soldiers.

*   *   *

As long as I could remember I had longed for a dog but Mother said that I must first be able to pay the 7s 6d licence myself. She had no intention of getting lumbered with a dog; she reckoned she had enough with Spats, and by setting me such an impossible task she had exonerated herself. The only dog with whom I was intimately acquainted was Rover, the guard dog at Grandad's farm. He was a huge black Newfoundland with a passion for swimming in the duck pond, the canal or any available stretch of water when he could get free, but mostly he was kept chained to his kennel in the yard. Intelligent animals become very bored in such circumstances but Rover had a friend with whom to pass the time, a little speckled hen who was cruelly persecuted by her companions; she took refuge in his kennel and roosted happily on his broad curly back. They became very devoted and she paid her rent every morning in the shape of a warm brown egg which he devoured with gusto. I wrote a little story about this unusual relationship and when I sent it to Dad's 'Daily' they printed it on the children's page and rewarded me with 7s 6d.

Mother was not amused but would never go back on her word for she abhorred liars; God, she said, kept a big black book in which to record my every lie so that when the day of judgement came I could be called upon to answer for them all. But what about the fibs made unknowingly? Did they count too? I started with judicious foresight to safeguard myself by muttering 'I think' after everything I said. People began to notice and often clouted me because they thought I'd said something else; you just can't win. However I did win over Spot who came to us as a tiny brown and white

29

pup and blossomed into a belligerent brute who put terror in the hearts of all who came within his orbit. But to me he was a most wonderful companion and we had a secret place which surpassed all others as an adventure playground. Our hide-out was a wooded hilltop crowned by an ancient castle and situated in an area so vast that it could have contained all the children of the neighbourhood and still been a place of solitude.

Because it was a tram ride from home it never occurred to anyone that we should go there, but we had our own short cut through scrub and wasteland and there I was able to squeeze between the rusty railings which someone of stronger calibre had wrenched apart. Spot, wider in girth, needed a tug to get him through and growled protestingly from the depths of his offending belly, but once through the railings the magic began: trees of great height and greater age congregated to form a green canopy with their topmost branches, shutting out the sun, the rain and, with a bit of luck, God too.

Deep caverns gouged into the hillside added to the fascination. Primeval man was said to have inhabited these caves but no one had ever penetrated their depths and lived to tell the tale. Inquisitive and wilful children had been known to disappear without trace into their dark interiors and search parties never discovered their poor remains. Perhaps early man raised his family in the well-ventilated chambers at the entrance, with blazing fires for warmth and illumination and to keep wild beasts at bay, and maybe his children did as they were bid. Spot and I, sustained with a torch and a length of string which I tied to a tree outside, probed the inner darkness until our string ran out, and in these dank vaults, deathly still and with the constant sound of dripping water, I would shout aloud with all the force of my lungs and hear the sound rebound in a thousand voices as though I was one with all the children who had ever gone before.

To be able to bawl one's head off without fear of reprisal is a rare and wonderful thing to do. There should be soundproof places provided where one could let rip without being rounded up by the Noise Abatement Society or incarcerated by the mental health wallas.

Sometimes primly and by tram we embarked on family outings to my castle, entering the grounds very properly by the main gate but always pausing to view, with disapproval, the statue in the road outside. It was, said Father, one of the earls of Dudley who during a foreign tour had had the temerity to penetrate the harem of an Eastern potentate and had been caught; for commiting this sacrilege his ears had been cut off. At this juncture I demanded evidence, but the errant earl had grown his hair long enough to cover the mutilation, which Father said was proof in itself. After this lesson on licentiousness we followed the prescribed paths up to the castle; on my own excursions I never had time to get this far and so despite parental control it was pleasurable. Sometimes there were fêtes and once as a small child I remember, from the height of Father's shoulder, cheering the current debonair earl as he stood, top hatted and tailed, his scarlet lined cape billowing in the breeze, while behind him the night sky erupted with a thousand fireworks.

More often than not our excursions were summer picnics. As soon as the parents were established on the grass and before they could bid me nay, I made my escape to the treasures that never palled. The kitchen block with the dark red stain upon the ground which, according to the keeper, had been oozing for more than a hundred years and which nothing could erase. Pressing my palms upon the damp discoloration I took away evidence to ponder over; surely murder most foul had been committed here and this was the blood of an innocent crying for revenge. Next the gateway through which Elizabeth the Virgin Queen had ridden in 1575 and then, evading the keeper's eye, up the stone steps of the great tower, described by Chaucer's knight as

> The grete tour, that was so thikke and strong
> Which of the castle was the chief dongeoun.

and from where I could look down upon the courtyard and

the diminished figures of my family.

At last, aloof and lonely as a cloud, I could dream of Ansculf the Picard adventurer who began it all. He was the brigand leader of a lawless band from Amiens who shacked up with William the Conqueror in 1066 and when it came to dividing the spoils he plonked for our Dudley. I didn't visualize then the exotic animals who would come to take over my domain and make it their own famous zoo.

*   *   *

I really did have an Aunt Fanny and I loved her next best to my sister Hilda. She was a collector of lame ducks, undernourished clerics and delinquent children, and she believed there was good in everybody, even me. Consequently I fell over backwards to show her how right she was.

She doted on her son Jack but despaired of ever rearing him. Though he is now in his seventies with a quiverful of grandchildren, he was a cosseted child – she even grated his turkey rhubarb and blew sulphur powder down his throat if it showed the slightest sign of becoming inflamed. She and Mother shared their medical know-how and at the onset of winter both Jack and I wore a piece of camphor stitched in little bags and pinned to our vest; the camphor evaporated slowly and by spring had disappeared altogether, though we carried the aroma with us *ad infinitum* (and never suffered from moths!). If we had sore throats we had to wear our fathers' woollen socks, scarf-wise, to go to bed in (and the socks still had to be warm from their feet).

When Jack caught 'chin-cough' (whooping cough), he was taken to the chemical works, and made to inhale pitch and tar fumes, but when Hilda had it she was taken to the gasworks for her inhalations. I didn't catch it and so was deprived of this unique experience. Our favourite medication was a lump of sugar with a couple of drops of Friar's Balsam (Tinc. Ben. Co.); it was delicious to suck and secretly we still do.

Jack's greatest pleasure was watching the trains go by and

writing the numbers of the engines in his little book. Although I was three years his junior his mother believed he was always safe with me and so we spent many hours train spotting at Watery Lane crossing. It was of no interest to me but to please Aunt Fanny was my aim in life.

She was a very ardent churchwoman and Good Friday was our most miserable day of the year; even household chores were forbidden and any unavoidable 'suds' must never be tipped down the sink but carried out and thrown on the garden. Between bouts of church going we were expected to sit quietly and ponder on the agonies of the crucifixion. I was sure I would go up in Aunt Fanny's estimation if I could weep over it, but however hard I tried I could never shed a tear. Later in life at times of emotional crisis I had only to think of Jesus on his cross and lachrymation was a convenient impossibility.

Jack was still such a little boy when he was taken from us, for despite the flowers of sulphor, the socks and the inhalations he had inherited the family voice and was chosen to become a chorister at Lichfield Cathedral. It was too great an honour to be denied and though it must have broken his mother's heart to part with him, his years away at the cathedral school matured him and coloured his whole life.

*　　*　　*

I was sent to Wolverhampton. It was usual for pupils to be entered for any available scholarship, as their school took credit for the number of passes obtained. My friend Kathleen and I passed for the new Tipton secondary school; we were proud to be amongst its first students and kept walking in front of Mademoiselle so that we could say, 'Excusez-moi s'il vous plait,' and she would know we already had a smattering of French. The school was only ten minutes walk from home and even less from Aunt Fanny's, but when I had been there two weeks the other results were published revealing that I had been given the choice of either Dudley or Wolverhampton High Schools. Wolverhampton was reputed to be the best school in the Midlands and despite my protests Father was determined I should go there.

To add insult to injury, the Director of Education wished to see me because I had obtained three scholarships, and I was sent from school in company with a girl who was to be censured for picking pockets. When we arrived at the imposing 'Public Offices' the great man got us confused so she had a pat on the head and half-a-crown while I had a good ticking off and a threat of expulsion!

It was a time-consuming journey to my new school, necessitating both train and bus, and most of the girls were private pupils who took a dim view of us 'Scholarshipites'. I'm afraid I never really applied myself to my lessons after I went there, except for games, gym and contributions to the school magazine for which Paget, my House, was awarded points. This annoyed poor Father to whom mathematics and Latin were the criterion.

'Scribbling will get you nowhere,' he would cry, and I had to fulfil my creative urges under the bed-clothes at night with a torch and have never since been able to 'scribble' except in secrecy and with a sense of guilt. Sadly, when going through his personal effects after Father died we found all my old school magazines carefully hidden away.

CHAPTER THREE

— Going to the Dogs —

I WAS SIXTEEN when I went to the dogs. Mother saw me off at Dudley Port station, having provided me with a single ticket to London, five bob and a packet of egg sandwiches. I had eaten the sandwiches before I got to Birmingham.

It was wintertime and I wore my navy blue school coat and my gymslip with a jumper on top, so that despite the pleats it gave the impression of being a skirt. I had removed the badge from my school hat and turned up the brim at a rakish angle of which Mother did not approve.

Changing trains at Birmingham held no qualms for me after six years of travelling by rail to school, and once under way on the London express I had the exhilarating feeling of having severed the umbilical cord. However I had one last rite to attend to; as the train screamed its way to the Great Metropolis I made my way along the swaying corridor to the loo and bolted myself in. A notice forbade me to use it when the train was not in motion, another announced, 'Gentlemen please raise the seat,' to which some wit had added 'Not you Momma, sit down!' However I had not gone there for that purpose. Carefully, for there was little room for manoeuvering, I stripped off all my clothes then tightly rolled up my combinations and black woollen stockings and stuffed them in the bin provided. 'Coms' had been one of the abominations of my life and anyone who doesn't know what they are is indeed fortunate. I carefully avoided looking at myself for I had been taught

35

that the body was not to be so lightly exposed and as I stood there naked, shivering and ashamed, there came a hammering on the door and a male voice demanded that it should be opened. I stood aghast and wondered what Mother would say if she could see my predicament, but apparently it was the inspector wanting to see my ticket so I rummaged in my baggage until I found it and opened the door just a few inches for its inspection, then I dressed hastily, putting on the brown lisle stockings which were intended for Sundays. I had to retain my Liberty bodice or I would have had nothing to fasten them to, then I scuttled back to my carriage where I had time to review the sins which had brought me to this pass.

I had defied Father and had left school against his express wish that I should continue my studies and become a teacher. He was stunned, incredulous, and his rage was such that the very sight of me sent him into a near fit, so it was obvious to me that I must leave home, cut off without even the proverbial shilling. In the reading room of the local library, in a magazine called *The Lady*, I found the solution: 'Required. A young lady of school-leaving age, of Matriculation standard and being a communicant member of the Church of England, to become a companion kennelmaid to a Mrs Tee in Bucks.' A reference from the vicar was necessary and the job was mine.

Now I was on my way. The kennels were nineteen miles from London so I had to change trains once more and Mrs Tee had promised to meet me at her end. I was very hungry by now but feared my five bob would not extend to refreshment and a ticket to the suburbs. Surely I would be given a meal after my long journey? At last the train steamed into the little wayside station and my heart faltered – this was it. As I descended on to the platform a tall angular woman like a pterodactyl bore down upon me with shrill cries – 'Please God, don't let this be her. Please God, please!' – but she by-passed me to embrace a fellow pterodactyl and I breathed again. There was no one else but a small rather dignified person in a cloche hat waiting by the wicket gate; this must be her. I hurried forward beaming with relief, hand outstretched: 'Mrs Tee? How do you do? I'm Edith Humphries.' Her cold eyes raked my school hat and coat, the cheap fibre case, and her mouth was pursed like a cat's arse. She ignored my proffered hand but indicated I should follow her and, deflated, I obeyed. Perhaps I would have been better off with the pterodactyl.

Mrs Tee led me to a car parked in the station yard. Cars were then quite a rarity, lady drivers even more so, but she drove with great confidence and I was suitably impressed. At last she spoke: 'Your parents are either very ignorant or else very foolish to allow a girl of your age to come without first vetting the place.'

'But I'm used to travelling alone – ' I rushed to the defence of my parents but she cut me short: 'That's irrelevant. Have they never heard of White Slave traffic?' I giggled at the thought of becoming a white slave but she was not amused and remained silent for the rest of our journey.

The house was very imposing, standing in large grounds and with three garages, and the yapping of dogs heralded our arrival. Mrs Tee introduced me first to the 'puppy room', an extension of the house, brick built but very well ventilated with large windows; two sides were taken up with wire-fronted compartments in which the dogs were housed and each contained a dog bed with a lavender blanket, a zinc tray lined with newspaper and a water bowl. Her puppy room, she told me, was much admired and had indeed had a write-up in *Our Dogs*. She had thawed visibly in these congenial surroundings and it was obvious how delighted the dogs were to see her. There were about thirty in all and over each was a card bearing their kennel name.

To me a dog is a dog and a mongrel as endearing as any aristocrat, but of all the thoroughbreds I think the most delightful, intelligent and enchanting is the Griffon Bruxellois and these were griffons. They eyed me speculatively with their quaint quasi-human faces while Mrs Tee introduced me to them. There was Partridge Hill Polyanthus, kennel name Polly, her original griffon, rather large and now an established brood bitch with many promising progeny to her credit; Blackbird, another brood bitch similar to Polly but with a harsh black coat whereas Polly's was 'red' or a rich rusty brown. Next came Beetle, a daughter of Blackbird but quite unlike her mother in that she was very tiny with a smooth coat like black silk; she was too small for breeding but was well known as a show dog and had the arrogance of a sleek duchess. Monkey, a rangy bitch with a face like a worn-out lavatory brush, was no beauty but she was nestling four adorable little pups. She was an excellent mother, said Mrs Tee, and when mated to a small but proven stud produced litters ideal to sell as pets. Mating was a function on which I hoped to improve my education; there had been much speculation at school on this dicey subject, for everyone conspired to preserve our so-called innocence, sex education was unheard of, and questionable parts of the anatomy ignored. Our head-mistress, a terrifying Dutch lady with legs like tree trunks, instructed us in Scripture, and one bold girl for a dare once asked her what circumcision was. After a stunned silence 'Miss' boomed: 'It is a nick in the part of the body in which the boy differs from the girl!' and mentally reserved the bold one for future persecution.

I knew better than to expose my ignorance to Mrs Tee who was extolling the virtues of a black puppy, one of Blackbird's last litter; she had high hopes for him at Crufts where puppies were then admitted and could compete in any adult class, but then she sighed, one could never be sure. Sunny, with his rich rust-red coat, his small beautifully set ears, his ideal nose and round dark eyes, his supreme confidence in the ring had swept the board only to put on a spurt of growth at twelve months and was now too big for show or stud and would soon be too old to be sold as a pet. Sunny listening with his head on one side knew he was under discussion but not approved of and looked very mumchance.

How had I come to apply for the job asked Mrs Tee, and when I explained that I had come across her advertisement in the reading room of the library the effect was electric.

'You mean' she cried, 'that your mother doesn't actually take *The Lady*?' And when I revealed that Mom only took *Home Chat*, her brow was thunderous and she stuttered that it was tantamount to deceit and I realized what a bloomer I had made. She had advertised in *The Lady* to get a lady and that I was not. Hurriedly she left me with a list of simple jobs to do and said she must prepare a meal for when Mr Tee arrived home at 7.30 p.m. By now I was ravenously hungry but deemed it would not be ladylike to say so. Left alone I took Sunny from his compartment and hugged him.

'I think we're both in the doghouse, old man' I said, and he snuggled ecstatically against me.

Mr Tee, who was something in the City, was a man of few words but I never knew him to be anything but kind. We had jugged hare for dinner, so revolting to my unsophisti-cated palate that I could eat only the vegetables. Mrs Tee commented tartly upon this for she said it was their favourite dish, and fearful of giving offence I excused myself by saying I was not fond of meat, a great mistake for from then on I didn't get any. The sweet was a mini-portion of pastry and the biscuits and cheese served only to Mr Tee.

After helping with the dishes I let the dogs out for a last run before bedding them down. Earlier I had fed them with minced meat mixed with Winalot, a new product which Mrs Tee said was very nutritious. There was a sack of it in the puppy room cupboard and I transferred a handful to the pocket of my brown holland overall, one of three which I had been instructed to bring. It was then nine o'clock and Mrs Tee told me I could go to bed. It was a dismissal but I was glad to go. It was very cold in my little room and I regretted the coms and black stockings which I could have worn under my nightie. Eventually I went to bed in my dressing gown and, because I was still very hungry after so meagre a meal, munched Winalot as I thought longingly of home.

Mr Tee roused me at 6.30 a.m. the following morning. My first job was to let the dogs out; they had a large lawn on which to run just outside the puppy room and very well fenced. Armed with a bucket and trowel I collected the turds and buried them at the bottom of the garden. There must never be evidence of these for visitors to see; dogs tend to favour the same spot for evacuation if possible and can easily be coerced to use their own territory, especially if there is a little mound of sand or similar material on which to perform. If away from home on two-day shows our dogs would usually only urinate and on their return we gave them a little boiled liver which encourages the process of elimination.

Meanwhile Sunny had taken on a proprietary air towards me, staying close and trying to keep the other dogs at bay. He began to stalk round me in ever-decreasing circles, standing tall and stiff-legged, his coat bristling; when he was close enough to touch he cocked his leg and ever so slightly wee'd on my ankle. The other dogs stood watching this ritual, recognizing that he was staking his claim to me.

I had my breakfast, porridge followed by a slice of bread and marmalade, at eight o'clock after the Tees had finished theirs. I hungered for more bread but feared to add a voracious appetite to my other shortcomings. At nine o'clock Lizzie the maid-of-all-work arrived; she was about my own age but with the advantages of a tight perm, curves and Californian Poppy. Mrs Tee objected to the latter and Lizzie promised not to use it again. She didn't; next day it was Phul-nana. She was not a girl to be intimidated.

As soon as we were alone she told me her name was really Shirl but that all well-off folk called their skivvies Lizzie. Well-off people, she added, were well off because they were so mean. This didn't worry her, however; it was a convenient job because she only lived in the village and all she needed was a reference which would open the doors to higher establishments.

'That's all you'll get at the end of twelve months,' she said, 'but no pay for you. The "young ladies" work for their bed and board.' She sniggered a bit over the 'board', then added, 'Of course they get their allowances from home.' This was news to me; certainly money had never been mentioned in my contract and there would be no allowance from home for I would never tell them I'd been fool enough to take a job for which I wasn't paid.

As the days passed Mrs Tee proved to be a hard taskmaster but a good teacher and I was most anxious to learn. As with Parkinson's Law 'Work expanded to fill time' and there were no spare moments. The dogs were supposed to have a brisk half-hour's walk daily and I took them, four at a time, armed with my trowel; it was not necessary but it showed willing and no dog however well trained is infallible. I enjoyed the walks though they were not as 'brisk' as they should have been because so many people stopped to admire my charges who reciprocated the attention for they were all proper little show-offs. Unfortunately the excessive exercise only increased my appetite which was now never assuaged, and the bag of Winalot diminished daily.

*　　*　　*

Amongst my new acquaintances were a couple who lived in the house on the hill. I took them to be father and daughter but Lizzie said they were husband and wife who had twin boys at boarding school. He was a retired RN captain and she was an ex-chorus girl with 'IT' and oodles of 'oomph'.

Lizzie and her contemporaries promoted the modern jargon and were slaves to fashion. In pursuit of the popular boyish look they wore tight calico binders round the chest to flatten their boobs. Edwardian ladies had their lower ribs removed to attain a waist small enough for a man's hands to span, and even Grandmother had worn a bustle, a little cage which she fixed over her posterior, securing it with tapes round her waist and draping her skirts over the contraption. Mother and my cruelly corseted aunts accentuated their busts and bums to emulate a figure 'S'. As a child I prayed 'Please God let me grow up quite square,' but he hadn't listened for here I was looking just like a beanstalk. Now my newest aunt, recently married to Mother's youngest brother, was a "flapper",' she wore knee-length low waisted skirts over pink silk stockings and had her hair shingled. Her prowess at the local Palais was such that the MC always chose her to demonstrate the latest dances; the uncles said John was a lucky chap.

Sometimes I met the captain's 'oomph' girl out riding in a most fetching get-up: hard hat, hacking jacket, polo-neck jumper and jodhpurs. Those I did covet; perhaps Mrs Tee would like me better if only I didn't look such a frump.

I would have been starved of affection had it not been for Sunny, but his devotion to me grew daily and though I was careful not to show any favouritism I recognized an extra-sensory perception which I had experienced before with animals, though not to such a degree. When I had my half-day once a week Mrs Tee allowed me to take him out with me and we explored the area, sometimes getting as far as the playing fields of Eton or Stoke Poges where the Prince of Wales went to play golf. More often, however, we came home in time for tea because I just couldn't afford to miss it, and then I carried on with my usual evening work for there was nothing else I really preferred to do.

One of the attractions of leaving home had been to escape church, but Mr Tee was warden of the local church and my attendance was a must. I resented my threepenny collection for by now the remains of Mother's five shillings were reduced to a few coppers and I was wondering what excuse I could make when it was revealed that I had nothing to put on the plate. However I was spared that ignominy by a postal order from Hilda, for though I had not made known my poverty she had guessed I would be hard-up. Her own income was small, for in 1931 teachers had taken a voluntary cut in salary to help the country's economy. I spent part of my postal order on cheese for which, like Ben Gunn, I had acquired a craving. I munched a small piece every night with my Winalot and never was there a more delicious bedtime snack.

Because of Mr Tee's parochial responsibilities we often

entertained ecclesiastical gentlemen, even a sprinkling of bishops. Mrs Tee was an accomplished hostess and in my capacity of 'companion' I was expected to converse with them. Here I was never at a loss for I found these dour theologians usually had a hidden streak of humour and were especially appreciative of Latin quips, and for the first time I blessed Father for his gift of a good education.

Meanwhile the thoughts of the canine fraternity were turned towards Crufts, the show of the year. Entrants now are hand-picked and must be proven winners, but fifty years ago this was not so and every kennel worth its salt hoped to participate. The breeders tended to gravitate together in order to find out who was showing what and to ascertain the opposition their own dogs would be up against. They were mostly shrewd, affluent women and there were several titled ladies amongst them. When we had a gathering there was much speculation about another breeder of griffons who never came up for air and seldom entered her dogs for shows, though she owned some of the best in the land. This mysterious lady was the Honourable Mrs Ionides. It seemed she kept her choice animals for her own satisfaction and she could afford to, for since inheriting the Shell millions she was the richest woman in the world. She was a friend of Queen Mary and also her personal 'adviser' in old china; obviously a lady to be cultivated. Nothing is more frustrating to a gaggle of women than the voluntary seclusion of another, for none of them had sight or sound of her. When approached she was never available and matters of breeding were dealt with by her subordinates. My admiration for her was boundless.

Mrs Tee had decided to enter Squeak, a young cobby little dog with an impressive beard and side whiskers and a beautiful coat, a potential stud if he could win three championship certificates and so become a champion. It was advisable to choose the best possible stud to mate (here we go again) your bitch; a second or third-class bitch like Monkey could be used for breeding but a doubtful dog was only a 'passenger' to his kennel, not even earning his keep,

43

whereas a good stud could make a fortune for his owner, commanding up to £10 for each service. Poor Sunny was a passenger, like a rejected child in an orphanage, for all who came to buy pets wanted a pup rather than an adult dog.

Belga too was to be shown for the first time; she was a shy endearing little bitch with all the right qualifications. She had been on heat once, but ideally bitches were not serviced until their second, and they came on heat roughly every six months; so far none of the others had done so and I was no nearer learning the facts of life. I bet Lizzie knew, but I wasn't going to ask her and lay myself open to ridicule, though she did say once that if a fella kissed you it was advisable to keep your lips tightly closed.

I couldn't see anyone wanting to kiss me.

Black Beetle was also one of the chosen, and of course the cherished Chough. Sometimes Mrs Tee had them in the house with her so that they would become compatible and confident in each other's company. A sudden scrap resulting in a torn ear or damaged nose would mean kaput, though I understand now that show dogs are allowed honourable scars without being disqualified.

It would be a good idea, said Mrs Tee, if I exercised the Crufts entrants together to encourage them to step out in a spritely manner, for their demeanour in the show ring was of paramount importance and Beetle, the old trouper, could be relied on to set a good example. Thus it happened that one day as we passed the house on the hill Mrs 'Captain' was entertaining some friends in the garden and she called them over to admire my select quartet. Suddenly there was a flurry as an outsize bull terrier belonging to the visitors leapt the gate and with menacing growls bore down upon us. There was time for nothing but to fall flat over my charges and endeavour to cover them, and they huddled close beneath me recognizing their danger. There was a rending of my nether garments and I parted company with my old gymslip; my little fingers, always vulnerable in a dog fight, were mauled before our attacker sank his teeth into my arm and at least while they were there the griffons were safe. I was conscious of a confusion of voices and feminine squeals above me when the situation took a dramatic turn as the captain strode upon the scene. He took a firm grip upon the bull terrier's broad studded collar while with the other hand he firmly but without injurious force squeezed its testicles. With a gasp the dog released me and as the captain bore it away he grinned into his abundant beard. 'A sure way of making anything loose its hold,' he said, adding another tip to my training.

They insisted on taking us indoors to clean me up and commiserate over my clothing. The bite on my arm was mainly bruising; only one tooth had penetrated the flesh and I still carry the scar. Then they took us home to explain to Mrs Tee whose concern was naturally for the dogs, but they were quite unharmed. Before she left Mrs Captain invited Sunny and I to tea on my next half-day. What a tea that was! I didn't need my Winalot snack that night. Mrs C said she'd had a new riding outfit and wondered if I would accept her old one in lieu of any damaged clothes. When I saw myself in the cheval mirror in her bedroom clad in the hacking jacket, jodhpurs and boots, I couldn't credit the transformation. Until then clothes had been purely functional; now I saw what they could do even for me. She was equally delighted and suggested cutting my hair; she had always trimmed that of her fellow chorus girls backstage. Before I fell from grace Father had cut mine by the expediency of putting a large basin on my head and cutting round it. Now remembering my flapper Aunt Elsie I asked if I could have a shingle. We'd go one better, she cried. I should have a bingle, the latest 'boyish look'. In one afternoon that darling girl completely changed my image.

I couldn't wait to show myself off. Mrs Tee smiled about once a week and she did so now. She wouldn't be ashamed of me at Crufts after all, and even her husband had the suspicion of a twinkle in his eye. He would be home on the great day, helped by Lizzie to attend to the dogs' essentials, but there would be no walkies.

It was a cold March morning when we set off for Crufts. I

sat in the back of the car with the dogs, but they travelled
well and wore little knitted coats in the lavender which was
their kennel colour, and under my hacking jacket I had a
polo-necked sweater of the same shade which Hilda had
made for me. Dogs and their owners were converging from
all directions. Most had travelled many miles or stayed
overnight; we were fortunate in being so accessible. Despite
the numbers there was a controlled excitement and the dogs
were surprisingly restrained. Each entrant had its own
number and stall and most had brought blankets in their
kennel colour to ensure comfort during the long hours of
waiting before and after judging took place. The public had
not yet been admitted and each breed was in its own little
group. By now I knew many of the breeders and I saw them
eyeing my new get-up. Trousers were not worn by women,
it just wasn't done, but jodhpurs – they were class,
smacking of hunting, gymkhanas and point-to-points. I
tossed my cropped head and felt very superior.

The great hall was like an indoor market: dog foods of
every description were on sale as were coats, beds, feeding
bowls and everything designed for the pampered pet;
though from the outlandish garments and booties and
diamanté collars these were purchased by pampered owners
for their own satisfaction. I cannot abide an animal to be
stripped of its natural dignity, as with the large poodle, a
mass of fur over the shoulders while its poor hind quarters
and vulnerable area over the kidneys are clipped bare,
exposed to the elements, and to add insult to injury an
idiotic pom-pom on the tip of the tail.

Mrs Tee said that until recently griffons had their ears
cropped to make them very small and upstanding but it was
now illegal, though still practised on the continent, and
some established show dogs were disqualified for the
mutilation. Griffon Bruxellois, as the name indicates, is a
Belgian terrier type of dog with short coarse hair. Griffon
means rough; there is also a smooth variety, correctly called
Brabançons. Our Beetle was one of these, though both her
parents were rough and also her litter companions. It's a

matter of luck what you get and until the coat grows you can't tell, but they all have the same delightful personality.

While waiting for the judging to begin we gave the dogs a final grooming; their coats were in peak condition for they had been 'plucked' some time before in order that they should be at their best for the show. Their coats were never clipped or cut and plucking was a tedious job; it consisted of pulling out the coarse top coat between thumb and forefinger, exposing the rich short undercoat which was at its best when it had grown a little. The dogs didn't object to this treatment but then they welcomed anything which relieved the tedium of kennel life. Next we turned our attention to the all-important beards and side whiskers which we combed with white of egg. It stiffened them and made them stand out to advantage. Belga alone objected to this and insisted on rubbing them against her stall and getting all mussed up. Beetle required no special attention for smooths are without whiskers, and her beautiful satin coat needed only a polish with a silk handkerchief (if you favour a sleek hairstyle this is a good tip to produce a gratifying sheen).

The public had now been admitted and the judges had arrived. Belga and Beetle were both entered for the first class for bitches. Neither Belga or I had been in the show ring before and so Mrs Tee decided to show Belga herself, leaving Beetle to me. I had been well versed in what I must do: stand still with Beetle on the ground showing to her best advantage, stand her on the table for examination, then run her in a straight line both towards and away from the judge; next the run round the ring with Beetle on the inside. It was most important that she should always be between me and the judge and that I must never speak to the judge unless spoken to first. How often we had practised all this but Beetle knew the drill without being prompted; she was nearly three years old, the peak for a smooth, and she had been performing in show rings for the greater part of her life. She was superb. Not so Belga. The alien atmosphere disturbed her profoundly; she cowered, she cringed, she

squatted on her haunches and refused to budge. In vain Mrs
Tee coaxed her. Eventually the judge waved them away and
turned to the next entrant. They returned to the bench in
ignominy. Poor Mrs Tee! The fact that Black Beetle took a
first did little to lessen the hurt; she'd had such high hopes
for Belga. But there was no time for agonizing, for soon it
was the class for Squeak and Chough. Squeak took a third
but Chough, the untried, took the place by storm; against
formidable odds he was proclaimed first every time and he
performed with the aplomb of his older sister Beetle.

When it was disclosed that a nine-month-old puppy was
taking precedence over the champions there was a general
exodus from the other rings where judging was in progress
and the crowds gathered round ours. Chough's jauntiness
and personality won them all and he accepted their
applause as being his due. When in the final class of both
bitches and dogs he was proclaimed champion of his breed
Mrs Tee was at the centre of a congratulatory crowd, and
while she was thus engaged I took the other three outside for
some exercise. They were feeling neglected and poor Belga
was in need of comfort.

Those of us in charge of dogs had a pass which entitled us
to come and go with them for obvious reasons. There was a
rather nonchalant young fellow walking gundogs; he too
wore riding togs with a dashing burgundy cravat striped
with blue. He looked across at me. The first compliment
anyone can pay you is to give you a second glance and he did
just that. Soon he came over and introduced himself as
'Spider' Webb. I reciprocated by saying my name was
Humphries and left it at that; the fewer folk who knew the
other the better. He was a groom, for his establishment bred
horses too and he described it enthusiastically; when we
parted it was with the promise of meeting on the morrow
for it was a two-day show.

When I returned to Mrs Tee officials were clearing a
passage through the crowd for an elderly man. It was
Charles Cruft himself come to congratulate her. I was so
overcome to see this great English showman I felt inclined to

bob a curtsy, but I was glad I didn't when he said to Mrs Tee, 'You have a fine kennel lad, M'am.'

Charles Cruft was then over eighty years old. When he was thirteen he entered the service of James Spratt, the dog biscuit manufacturer, and from that small beginning his main interest was the welfare of the canine species. He was thirty years in the service of Spratts, rising to become the general manager, but he organized his first dog show one hundred years ago in 1886 and because of his efforts the standard of breeding and the popularity of dogs has greatly increased. The lean war years for animals would have grieved him greatly had he not died, most opportunely, in 1939.

*   *   *

'Puppy wins Championship at Crufts' blazed the headlines of the London evening papers; such a thing had never happened before (and I don't think it has ever happened since). When we got home there was a message from Mrs Ionides. She wanted to buy Chough, but although Mrs Tee could name her own price she was not tempted. As his breeder and owner her reputation had soared; he had to win two more championships to become a full champion, but after such a start they were a foregone conclusion. I was longing to see him in the 'Best in Show' parade at the finale the following day and was acutely disappointed to find that Mrs Tee had decided to take advantage of the privilege accorded puppies which was that they need not attend on the second day. She was sure he stood no chance of becoming best in show and was overtired herself. I was to take the others on my own.

Griffons had no showing to participate in that day but many people came to see them and were disappointed to find Chough was not there. Beetle was very popular and several would like to have bought her for she had the same pedigree as Chough and was a joy to show, but Mrs Tee would never sell her for although she contributed nothing to the kennel but her reputation she was too small to breed

49

from and even if they promised not to, potential buyers might be tempted to do so. Small bitches sometimes need Caesareans or even die whelping. Mrs Tee would never subject Beetle to such a risk for she always put her dogs before monetary gain and neither would she sell her puppies to dubious buyers or families with very young children.

It was still quite early when a familiar voice hailed me with 'Hi legs!' and the name was to stick amongst the young fraternity for the rest of my dog days. It was Spider, of course, delighted to see that Mrs Tee had not turned up. He still had some showing to do for his were 'working dogs'. I thought he sounded a little superior about the working bit, as though no dog was worth its salt unless it was functional. Several of his contemporaries wandered over too and I noticed they all wore the blue and burgundy cravats which were the colours of their establishment. They said it was much better working as a group; the food was good and the pay reasonable, there were both grooms and kennelmaids but not enough of the latter to go round. Spider was sure he could get me placed if I'd a mind to go. I hadn't told him the terms under which I worked. I was supposed to stay with Mrs Tee for twelve months but I felt sure she would be glad to replace me with someone more congenial. Poor woman! My Blackcountry accent alone drove her to distraction. Spider said they led quite a social life too with high jinks and petting parties.

'O I should love that!' I cried and he looked at me with renewed interest. Fancy being able to keep your own pets! Immediately I thought of Sunny. Perhaps Mrs Tee would let me buy him if I sent her all my wages. I knew she would be pleased to get rid of him too if he was well placed. My head was whirling with new plans for both of us for the thought of ever parting with Sunny was unbearable.

Spider's mates and their dogs had travelled in a brake but he had a little red Morgan, a three-wheeler of which he was very proud, and he insisted on taking us home in it. It was certainly easier than public transport with three dogs, but I didn't dare ask him in. The next Kennel Club show was at the Crystal Palace and we planned to meet there.

*   *   *

My visit to the Crystal Palace would have been a novel and memorable experience even without the dogs. It was a mountain of light, so vast that exotic plants and even huge trees grew within its lofty enclosure. A large concert hall catered for musical festivals and everywhere statues of Greek gods, virile athletes and coy ladies in the altogether disported themselves. It had been the brain child of Sir Joseph Paxton, one-time gardener's boy, to accommodate Prince Albert's Great Exhibition of 1851 in Hyde Park, after which it was dismantled and rebuilt on the hill at Sydenham where the spaciousness lent scope for expansion.

This great Victorian enterprise, so beloved of royalty, was censured by many influential people. Shortly before the opening at Sydenham 'thirteen eminent persons' sent a letter condemning the licentiousness of the Greek statues and demanding 'the removal of the parts which in life ought to be concealed'. It was an 'or else' letter and the authors must have been powerful as well as eminent for the unhappy deities had to suffer the indignity of having their virility removed with hammer and chisel. Unfortunately there was a dearth of fig leaves and the plasterers hastened to provide cover for the emasculation before Queen Victoria opened the new Palace on 10 June 1854 in the presence of 40,000 people. Since then, however, generations of small boys had creatively contributed to the coverage and so embellished the shushies of the shy maidens so as to set the 'thirteen eminent persons' revolving in their graves.

When we had settled the dogs Mrs Tee gave me leave to explore the place and I did so with enthusiasm. By now I had made friends with many devotees of this canine cavalcade and I had a new love, Luscombes Melody, a beautiful whippet whom I visited whenever I got the chance. Melody's proud grace had won my heart. I felt very disloyal to the griffon fraternity to have found a breed I admired more, though of course my affection for Sunny was

51

undiminished. I loved him for himself alone and his own unquenchable character.

When I'd had my fill I went out into the sunshine to find the gardens as entrancing as the palace, for the hill on which it had been built was landscaped with great skill and the view from it was panoramic: white clouds scudded across a blue sky and beneath me the steep slope had been terraced with abundant flora. Spider who had been watching out for me had followed, anxious to impart the news that he had paved the way for me to join his establishment; all that remained was for me to make my peace with Mrs Tee. He was so tall with a cynical charm and I was filled with a strange elation; there was no one else in sight and we might have been standing alone on the edge of the world. He put his arm round my shoulders and tilted my face for a kiss, my first real kiss, and no place could have been more idyllic. Gently he bent his head at an angle and placed his lips on mine – so that was where the noses went, I'd often wondered! Deep within me a curious excitement began to stir, something such as I had never known before, and as if in response his kiss became more urgent and exploratory and with a practised hand he fondled my immature boobs. This was a liberty! Outraged, I gave him a hearty shove and he toppled backwards over the perimeter. It was a tidy drop and when I peered over he was sitting in a small pond, and on his face was an expression of extreme astonishment. When I was sure that nothing more than his pride was injured I hared me back to the shelter of Mrs Tee and didn't leave her again. If that was an indication of what to expect I'd finished with fellas and he could stuff his job.

* * *

Less than three years later Paxton's Palace was completely destroyed by fire on 6 November 1936. The army were *in situ* at the time and the conflagration was said to have started in a lavatory, but despite the efforts of eighty-nine fire engines the flames soon rose to 300 feet. Arson was denied, so how come 500 tons of glass and 9,642 tons of iron (not to mention the ubiquitous stone statuary) could be consumed in so short a time?

* * *

Belga had come on heat and it was for the second time, so Mrs Tee decided she should have a litter. It might give her more confidence and also she would be contributing something towards her upkeep. We had too many passengers. Squeak, a potential stud, had proved to be impotent and could now only be sold as a pet; unlike Sunny he was still the ideal size and so his future owner could continue to exhibit him, and that gave pride and satisfaction to many amateurs. But prize money won at shows, even for firsts, was not sufficient to cover expenses and entrant fees; publicity was the aim.

Belga's chosen mate was a top stud dog but, even more important, his pedigree was compatible with hers. It must be remembered that pups have grandparents, great-grand-parents and great-great-grandparents *ad infinitum* and that they are more likely to take on the characteristics of their forebears than those of their parents. Belga's stud served only approved bitches lest his name be smirched with unsatisfactory progeny and she had to be mated on the appropriate day and again two days later. It was so frustrating that I should be conversant with these intricacies of genetics and yet be ignorant of the fundamentals. I was anxious to take her but it was a good car journey away and Mrs Tee wished to be there herself for Belga was tempera-mental and, she insinuated, some breeders were unscrupu-lous enough to substitute another stud if the chosen one had several bitches to serve in a comparatively short time.

The right day for Belga coincided with the next show but only Chough and Beetle were entered and it was decided I should escort them. I had no wish to meet up with Spider and so stayed put in the area occupied by the griffon clique and looked around to assess what competition we were up against. I reckoned Mrs Mitchell's Simon of Lavenderway was Chough's closest rival; he was a fine cobby little dog, a rough black and tan who was two years older than Chough. But there were two dogs I hadn't seen before, good ones too, and when I looked in the catalogue it was revealed that they were from the Vulcan Kennels owned by the Honourable Mrs Ionides.

This was indeed fodder for investigation. Perhaps I could wheedle some of that elusive lady's secrets from her kennelmaid who looked large, lonesome and long in the tooth, so reminiscent of Bina that I longed to befriend her. You'd have thought her exalted mistress would have kitted her out in something smarter than that faded overall, but then she probably never saw her. When I asked about the well-known dogs who had been acquired by her kennels and not seen since, she said they had gone abroad, apparently to one of their mistress's overseas establishments. She was very forthcoming and I pumped her shamelessly. What a scoop! I heard myself relating it all to Mrs Tee when we returned. 'Have you ever actually seen Mrs Ionides?' I queried at last. An enigmatic smile flickered across her homely face.

'I am Mrs Ionides,' she said.

When one has committed the most flagrant *faux pas* and there is no redress only the prerogative not to panic remains, so I tried to keep my cool, to behave as though I rubbed shoulders daily with multi-millionairesses, scions of nobility, friends of queens. I thanked her for her most interesting conversation, I shook hands with her, and I beat it.

It was more difficult telling Mrs Tee and tell her I had to, for my sins always found me out and it was better to get my version in first. She was coldly furious. It was no more than she expected from one of my ilk. A letter of apology must be sent, though of course no acknowledgement could be expected. Acknowledgement, however, came in the form of a letter from Mrs Ionides's secretary stating that an apology was not necessary. Mrs Ionides had found my approach 'very refreshing' and when my term with Mrs Tee was finished I was welcome to apply to her for a job if I wished.

* * *

Hilda's postal orders kept me going in cheese, church collections and etceteras, and from time to time I received rather formal letters from home with postal stamps to ensure a reply. The bathroom scales were a novelty but I learned from them how much weight I had lost since I came. No wonder with all the exercise! Then all of a sudden my periods ceased; that however was convenient and saved me the 'etceteras'.

All the sex education I'd had from Mother was that when I had my 'Monthly' I must on no account wash my hair or get my feet wet and I had obeyed her implicitly, even to hanging my feet, by dint of much juxtaposition, over the edge of the bath during ablutions, so I knew I'd done nothing wrong, but it was a funny how d'you do.

I woke up one night as suddenly as if a brick had been dropped on my head. Of course – I was pregnant! That kiss Spider had given me! Girls at school had reckoned it all started with a kiss, and Lizzie had warned me to keep my lips closed tight if ever a fella kissed me. Staring into the condemnatory darkness I could see no comfort; I could never go home again. I'd heard of girls 'getting into trouble' and not only were they ostracized but their families were as well. I must just disappear and find myself a job, however menial, for which I was paid enough to keep my baby and myself. That I should part with it or tell Spider never occurred to me.

During the next couple of weeks I was hardly *compos mentis*. I even went off my Winalot and when Monkey came on heat Mrs Tee, noticing I was looking peaky, said I could take her to be serviced, a concession that was little consolation though it was a task I had long hankered after. Monkey was going to her usual mate owned by two spinster ladies at Maidenhead and I set off with her carrying a colourful blanket in case of emergency. I soon had to carry her because we had acquired a following of persistent dogs and she was quite heavy, so I was glad when we boarded the bus and were able to shake off her unwelcome admirers. We had to change buses at Slough and it was amazing how soon more dogs got wind of us. They were very quarrelsome amongst each other; some kept jumping up at me and I was jolly glad when we reached out destination. Mrs Tee's wisdom in taking the bitches by car was obvious.

The maiden ladies made us very welcome and took us to a room at the top of the house where we would be undisturbed. It was quite bare except for a strip of carpet on which they placed the dogs, 'to prevent them slipping, dear.' They were most solicitous about their precious stud; one took charge of him and one of Monkey lest they should inadvertently do each other a mischief. They needn't have been so concerned, for Monkey and her mate were obviously delighted with each other and in no time he had mounted her. I stared in amazement and only just managed to stifle a giggle. So this was what it was all about! Why, years ago when I'd seen animals in this ridiculous position, Mother had said they were 'being rude' and I must never watch. Could this really be the act of procreation? If so, I certainly wasn't pregnant and never would be I decided. Surely Mom and Dad had not participated in this act? I shied away from the idea. Some things were inconceivable, like with the King and Queen and Mr and Mrs Tee, but what a fool I had been and how thankful I was no one else knew it.

The two participators remained locked for a considerable time but they must never be forced apart said my companions, otherwise they could become ruptured. It was a good mating and they didn't think a second service would be necessary. Monkey was always so cooperative. It wasn't always as easy, especially with maiden bitches, but dear old Monkey, despite being over-large and certainly not show material, had an excellent pedigree and produced very desirable progeny, all of which were complimentary to their own little stud.

When it was over we went downstairs and they were very hospitable, but they were also anxious that I should nurse

Monkey on my lap for a while, her rear slightly upended to ensure that none of the precious sperm should go to waste. The dear creature lay on her back in happy abandonment, revelling in the rare attention, and it struck me that she contributed financially to the kennels more than any of the much lauded show dogs and – she had taught me the facts of life! Finally we escaped and I carried Monkey but I no longer felt her weight for I was walking on air with sheer relief.

At Slough we had missed our hourly connection by only a few minutes. It was pouring with rain and nothing could damp my spirits now, but I was concerned for Monkey and there was no place to shelter, so we went into a shoe shop and asked to see their selection. We were high and dry and they weren't to know that I had nothing more than the bus fare in my pocket. There were no other customers and I must have tried on every shoe of my size in the shop by the time our bus was due and I have felt a sense of guilt in shoe shops ever since.

* * *

We had a small room as far as possible from the other dogs, which was reserved for bitches on heat and those 'in pup' during the latter stages; their period of gestation is nine weeks and it is advisable fo familiarize them with their surroundings before whelping. About one week before Belga was due to whelp Mrs Tee took Chough to a championship show up north which meant, of course, that she had to stay overnight. Shortly after she left, Belga became restless and didn't want to be left alone, so I kept her with me while doing the chores. I wondered if she might be going into premature labour but I didn't tell Mr Tee when he came home because I knew that when she phoned him later he would feel bound to tell Mrs Tee about it and she would be so concerned. Also, I might be wrong, but I knew I wasn't when Belga began 'making her bed', scratching around and tearing up bedding with the primeval instinct of an animal making its nest.

57

Mrs Tee always attended to a whelping herself but if possible she allowed me to be present as part of my training: she also phoned the vet at the onset of labour to ensure he was available should there be any complications, not an unusual thing with griffons because of the large broad head, so I took the opportunity of doing this while Mr Tee was taking his bath. However with twilight a blanket of fog had descended and now visibility was almost nil and the vet, who lived a distance away, doubted he could make it even if it was necessary, so I was on my own. I had always wanted to do veterinary work, even hoped that by working at a kennels I might get in at the back door as an assistant or nurse, but all the veterinary surgeons I'd come across seemed to enlist their wives or teenage children for the job. Now was the chance for some first-hand experience: Belga had begun to strain and I prepared for a sleepless night.

There was an old armchair and the room was heated, for warmth was essential if the pups were to survive, especially any as premature as these. I prepared a box for them with a hot-water bottle well wrapped in a clean blanket and sterilized the surgical scissors used by Mrs Tee. At hand I had a roll of veterinary wool, disinfectant, a lubricant, covered bucket, towels and plenty of hot water. Although most breeds can deliver their pups unaided, few griffons are able to do so, partly because of the undershot jaw and partly because of the short foreface which makes it impossible for them to reach round their distended body to attend to themselves. Each pup is enclosed in its caul, a bag of membrane containing fluid, in which it is usually born as a complete, neat little package.

Belga's straining became more pronounced, and after about an hour the tip of the caul was showing as a small dark ball which was the head inside the membrane. It disappeared between each strain to appear with the next, but we didn't seem to be getting much further and Belga was getting tired, until I managed to get a grip on the shoulders and pull gently with each strain; I knew one must never pull on the head, of course. Finally the pup came away, trailing its afterbirth behind it. I could feel it struggling in the little grey bag and hastened to remove the caul from over its face, whereupon the tiny mouth opened to take its first breath. Quickly I cleansed the face and nostrils and peeled off the membrane, cutting the umbilical cord about two inches from the fat little belly. It was now free and after rubbing it briskly in a warm towel I held it up to Belga's face for her to lick it. What a pity she had not been able to do all this herself as she should normally have done. When put to a teat it soon began to suckle, but when Belga began to strain again I popped it in the warm hot-water bottle box out of the way.

By morning there were four adorable puppies, each weighing three to four ounces, each with large heads and very dark coats, a breeder's dream. But they had all been difficult births and it struck me that had Belga gone full term they would have been that much bigger and consequently more hazardous. She accepted a bowl of warm milk and I tried to persuade her to eat the afterbirths which bitches do when delivering themselves, for they contain desirable nutrients for the mother and stimulants for the flow of milk.

When Mr Tee got up he was amazed to find that I had been up all night and that we had four new additions to the family. I had got his breakfast ready and he insisted I should share it with him and give an account of my nocturnal activities. His wife on her return was shocked, incredulous and gratified, in that order, to find Belga gloating over her little family, and four days later as a great concession she let me dock their tails and dew claws, albeit under strict supervision. Tail docking is an unnecessary mutilation but I have no qualms about the removal of dew claws for they are easily torn and can cause pain and distress to the adult dog, being situated at the base of the leg like a useless thumb but more often now only on the forelegs, as though Nature herself recognizes their superfluity. Belga's brood continued to thrive and I felt I had a special affinity with them.

*   *   *

Inexorably time had passed and my last day was at hand. I

hadn't been home for twelve months, less one week which I
was now having in lieu of annual leave, and this meant I
would be gone for Christmas. I was looking forward to that
for Hilda would be home too. Father had unbent sufficiently to send my fare. At least I had proved myself by staying
the full time but I felt I was a failure, for Mrs Tee's aversion
was almost a tangible thing. I had to admire her; she was a
lady of excellent qualities but she had never forgiven the
lapse of *The Lady*. I was the one out of step for we were
miles apart: every avenue of breeding was of paramount
importance to her; she was always harking back to her own
formidable forebears whereas I have always been content to
trace my ancestry to the first protoplasmic cell propagating
in primeval sludge.

I had worked hard; several breeders had offered me jobs —
and there was always Mrs Ionides! But I wondered if I was
in the right rut after all. What good did it do to breed
animals with abnormal characteristics? I had once seen a
weeping owner kneeling beside her champion bulldog
which was dying of a heart attack: the snub nose hampered
its breathing, the abnormally square chest pushed the heart
out of alignment and the excitement of the show had been
the last straw.

Meanwhile the new girl had been for an interview in a
stately automobile flanked by protective parents who
would undoubtedly cough up munificent pin-money. It had
become fashionable for young people with good back-
grounds to learn the ethics of breeding before setting up a
select little kennels of their own where, with good
connections, they soon acquired a lucrative clientele. This
young Miss still bore the aroma of an exclusive boarding
school and I could bet my bottom dollar her mother
subscribed to *The Lady*, but I couldn't see her as a gatherer
of turds!

To part with my charges was a great wrench but to leave
Sunny was heartbreaking, and I spent a sleepless night
shedding tears in the comforting darkness. I had let the dogs
out for a last run on the grass before leaving on the

afternoon train when the folks on the hill arrived to say goodbye. The Captain marched into the house and his wife said he had gone to buy Sunny for her. She had always been enchanted with him, ever since the memorable day when we had gone to tea, and I was so overcome I embraced her with a joy which could never have been expressed in words. Sunny stood watching, his head cocked characteristically on one side. I gathered him up and buried my face in his tawny, warm fur until I could control myself; our minds were as one and his apprehension was conveyed to me.

'Love her,' I pleaded silently. 'Love her as you have loved me and you will be happier than you have ever been.' I put him down before her and the look he gave me was one I will never forget. Then he gazed questioningly at his new mistress and as the other dogs watched he began his ritual, stalking round her in ever-decreasing circles, standing tall and stiff-legged, his coat bristling; when he was close enough to touch he cocked his leg and ever so slightly wee'd on her ankle.

CHAPTER FOUR

— Gathering Rosebuds —

HOME IS THE place where one can be ill without culpability, but it wasn't until I arrived there that anyone realized I was ill.

I'd had a spate of boils and a painful swelling in my thigh which now blossomed into a huge abscess so that I had to take to my bed, have it lanced and suffer the application of scalding bread poultices. I had never before been visited by a doctor and Sybil, a family friend who had been a nurse before her marriage, came to dress my leg. She was an endearing little person with a country-girl complexion, rich brown hair and a year-old son. Since Cecil I'd had an antipathy to doctors and nurses but Sybil changed all this. She spoke nostalgically of her nursing days, of the companionship of other girls, of job satisfaction, and she wooed me to follow in her footsteps.

First, however, I must have a clean bill of health. When it was revealed that I was also suffering from malnutrition, my parents were shocked and mortified and Mother went to work on me with Iron Jelloids, Parrishes food and Pink Pills for Pale People, but despite these I made a speedy recovery and under Sybil's guidance began making applications to suitable establishments.

When I was accepted at Standon Orthopaedic Hospital, a two-hour train journey from home, Sybil approved. I was anxious to escape, for the vicar, who erroneously imagined I was good missionary material, was making fresh overtures.

Mother and Dad saw me off with obvious relief and loud exhortations to chastity. It was 15 May 1934.

I was wearing a camel hair coat, a small hat and matching scarf, gifts from Hilda. I regretted that my beloved breeches were redundant, but little did I realize how great the demand for them would be, for both hospitals in which I was to serve encouraged amateur theatricals and they were the ideal garb for licentious Lotharios, dashing dandies and dissolute country squires.

I had to change trains at Stafford and get the local train to Crewe, and when I disembarked at Standon I was gratified to find the matron's car awaiting me, chauffeured by a likeable chap who explained he was her general factotum. On the two-mile trip along country lanes he explained this was a service provided for all newcomers, lest the long jaunt to the hospital so deterred them that they turned tail and took the next train home. They would have had a long wait for there were only two trains a day, the next being an evening express which deigned to pause briefly, solely for the benefit of the nursing staff. On Sunday and Wednesday afternoons two coaches conveyed visitors from outlying areas; if you were lucky you could get a lift, but not of course a return trip.

The hospital had only been opened two years previously and consisted of a lovely old Hall, once occupied by a titled gentleman, and two large open air pavilions, North and South, in which the wards were situated. A little distance from the pavilions and connected by covered corridors was a large, very modern theatre block.

All this was approached by a long winding driveway flanked by colourful rhododendron bushes and terminating in a courtyard where it was customary for the local hunt to meet. On this May morning it looked very beautiful.

I was ushered into matron's presence and thanked her for the use of her car. She accepted me graciously, unlike the attendant home sister who had the task of kitting me out in uniform. I was, she said, quite the wrong shape. She went to

63

work on me with a tape measure but dismissed my vital statistics as 'two yards of single width'. I was not concerned; curves were not 'à la mode'. Something, she said, must be done about my hair. It was not quite 'suitable' and none must show from under the starched white cap; fringes or bangs were considered to be 'fast' and must be pinned back until they had grown. The ankle-length dresses with three deep tucks at the hem were of a harsh blue and white striped material and lined with calico. The long sleeves had six white buttons with button-holes from wrist to elbow; the elbow itself bore a seventh button minus a button-hole. This, explained the home sister, was to provide a sharp and painful reminder should any nurse be so injudicious as to lean her elbows on the table.

A dozen starched white aprons were added to the dresses, plus a laundry bag, stiff white cuffs and collars, and matching belts. The smallest size in belts was a twenty-six. I was twenty-two, and so they swung about my waist like hoops until I learned to bodge holes in their immaculate surface and adjust the studs. The collars were high and rigid and wore a line of demarcation round the neck, so that when off-duty we looked like refugees from a chain gang.

I had already been instructed to bring with me black woollen stockings, flat rubber-heeled ward shoes, a watch with a second hand and a pair of blunt-ended scissors. With all my new gear stowed away in the laundry bag, home sister propelled me before her into the dining hall. It was filled with chattering nurses, but simultaneously the prattle ceased and all eyes swivelled towards us. On each of the three large tables was a loaf of bread, a basin of jellied dripping and a bottle of brown sauce. Huge enamel jugs of cocoa completed the repast.

Sister introduced me briefly. I was, she instructed, to be taken to my room to unpack, and then at two o'clock I was to report for duty on North pavilion. She handed me over to a pimply nurse with brown smears on her apron, who apparently was to be one of my room-mates. 'I hope, Nurse

Jennings,' she said, pointing to the smears, 'that those are nothing more than sauce!' Then she made a dignified exit and Nurse Jennings stuck out a tongue at her retreating back.

I was given a chair and a cup of strong, sweet cocoa, but I declined the bread and dripping annointed with sauce, though I later found it to be delectable and do so until this day. Meanwhile, my companions continued to devour it with voracity, their chatter renewed doublefold.

Slowly sipping cocoa, I tried to follow their discourse, but so many words were quite alien to me. Some, I was sure, were not quite nice. I did, however, make a wonderful discovery: surnames only were used. All my life my Christian name had been a pain in the neck, but I was no longer 'our Edie!' Henceforth I was 'Humphries!'

Later, I was to work for years with girls, share their bedrooms, their stockings, their innermost secrets, and part still not knowing their Christian names. Some were followed by younger sisters, but even then the custom was adhered to by the sisters themselves. Big Kelly and Little Kelly, Big Potter and Little Potter. The fact that in stature the little ones were bigger than the big ones made no difference. Big merely meant senior.

Inevitably, two o'clock arrived. Nurse Jennings delivered me to the sister of North pavilion, who directed me to the boys' ward. 'You had better,' she said, 'get on with the round.'

Boys! I had no brothers; I knew nothing of boys. Apprehensively, I entered the ward. Thirty pairs of eyes viewed me speculatively, seeing fodder for fun! The nearest boy demanded a bottle and immediately all the others took up the call. Relieved, I went in search of bottles. At least this was something I understood. I soon located the kitchen and put on all the available kettles to heat. Searching the cupboards, I found a pile of hot water bottles and was hastily filling them when sister tracked me down. Wordlessly, she took me by the ear and led me to the sluice; pointed to a rack of strange receptacles and bellowed in my now painful ear: 'Bottles!' She then pointed to even stranger vessels: 'Bedpans!' She indicated a large sink with a hole in the middle over which a lavatory chain was suspended. 'You empty them there!' Abruptly, she left me.

The boys were now calling more urgently and they wanted bedpans too. Most of them lay recumbent on iron frames, or else were encased in plaster. They were very heavy and awkward to lift. Incredibly, I had reached that stage of my life without ever seeing a nude male apart from the emasculated statues of the Crystal Palace. Decorously, I averted my eyes, fumbled under the bedclothes and pushed the bedpans in, all of course the wrong way round! The results were calamitous. Even with the help of the other nurses, it took hours to clean up the boys and readjust them on their splints. Toilet paper was not used in those days, instead a horrible hairy stuff called 'tow', which had afterwards to be burned. The patients happened to be on a course of sulphur tablets as well and the stench was terrible. I was very unpopular and had to spend the whole evening washing out sheets.

I shared a bedroom with four other girls, but I was so tired I hardly noticed them. At 6.30 a.m. the following morning I was abruptly roused by night sister stripping the bed (none of us had heard the awakening bell so we all got the name treatment). There was a general scramble to get washed and dressed and in the dining room for seven o'clock. I was warned by my room-mates to beware of 'Calamity', the night sister, who was, so they said, an unholy terror. If you didn't eat all your breakfast she gave you an aperient. Trembling, I entered the dining room just as the clock struck seven. Night sister, a terrifying spectacle with bright yellow hair, was doling out porridge to each customer. She handed me a great dollop and I acknowledged it courteously. 'Thank you, Sister Calamity.'

A stunned silence ensued. The other nurses stared fixedly at their porridge but night sister withered me with a searing glare. 'Kindly leave the room!' she boomed, and I crept out still carrying my porridge. For the rest of my time there, she ruthlessly persecuted me.

Back on duty, ward sister watched me like a hawk and was just as merciless. First I had to pull out all the beds so that the wardmaid could clean behind them, and many were elevated at the foot on heavy iron contraptions, just to bawk me. By the time they were all back *in situ*, I was quite exhausted. Next, I was commandeered by the senior nurse for bedmaking; she was brisk and Irish and rather faddy about 'envelope corners'. She left all the lifting to me and I had an awful job to keep up with her.

When we reached a boy who only had both legs splinted and was able to sit up, he complained that his bottom was sore. Senior nurse turned on me as I came up at a trot, panting and flushed. 'You!' she cried. 'Go and get an airing!' How kind I thought, she really was quite human after all. Gratefully, I went out in the grounds and sat under a tree; cool breezes soothed my fevered brow.

I was amazed when someone came in search of me. How was I to know she meant an air-ring?

The off-duty period consisted of two free hours a day and one free day a fortnight; today was the day on which ward sister made out the rota for the next two weeks. She booked my day off for the following day. I had not dreamed of getting it so soon, but doubtless she had reasons of her own. She sent for me and explained that a day off was always preceded by an evening off-duty to enable nurses within living distance to spend the night at home. I would, therefore, finish duties when the bell rang for second tea. If I were to forgo my tea I would just have time to catch the evening train. She seemed very anxious I should get the train. Perhaps she was hoping I would not come back.

Consequently, at 5.30 p.m. I hurried to my room, shed my uniform and once again donned mufti. The last day and a half had seemed endless and it was strange to be wearing ordinary clothes again. Then I set off at a steady pace for the station. It seemed a very long two miles and the express and I arrived simultaneously. It gave a shrill snort of disgust at having to halt for one solitary passenger and I barely had time to embark before we were on our way.

I had the carriage to myself, and as we sped through the countryside I wondered what sort of a reception I would get at home. They would naturally be taken aback by my premature appearance, but if I did not go it might be as long as a month before I had another day off. Then they would be suspicious, and want to know what I had done with my time and the return fare they had given me. It was all a bit of an anti-climax.

The next stop was at a main-line station, and this time the wait was a long one. When I asked a passing porter, he explained that the Scottish express had been delayed and that unless we stayed for it, many of its passengers would miss their connections.

Just then it steamed in at the adjoining platform and there was a general exodus. Porters rushed people and their baggage across to my train, and in the affray two of them bundled a young man into the carriage with me. He seemed rather reluctant, but they threw his luggage in after him, slammed the door and, with a shriek of protest at the delay, the train moved off, bent on making up for lost time.

The young man looked around with obvious dismay and then began to pace the floor in great agitation. He was a very presentable chap, but I mentally gauged the distance between myself and the communication cord. He paused momentarily to ask how long it was before the next stop, and when I told him it was about half an hour he groaned aloud and perspiration beaded his brow. Anxiously, I asked if he was ill and then, continuing his capers, he told me. It was all so simple really; he had boarded the other express hours previously but his compartment had no corridor; neither had this. Could he possibly make use of the window? 'Of course!' I cried, turning my back towards him.

Urgently, he made for the opposite door and let down the window. Looking at my end of the carriage it struck me he would be needing very long legs! There was the sound of much scrabbling. He appeared to be climbing on to the seat, and, against the gathering darkness outside, I saw his reflection in my window. He was astride the seats like a Colossus.

After a considerable time he descended, re-arranged himself and in some confusion thanked me. 'Don't worry,' I beamed 'you don't have to feel embarrassed with me. You see,' I added with pride, 'I'm a nurse.'

* * *

It was now over three weeks since I had been let loose upon the world of nursing. I had not yet had a second day off. When returning from the first, I had boarded the rear portion of the train and for some inexplicable reason (except that I was on it!), this part was later unhitched from its counterpart and taken to a different part of the country, leaving me stranded late at night in alien territory.

When I failed to return to the hospital no one was surprised; they decided I had just done a bunk. Ward sister was elated and night sister justified, but when I returned after midnight with a police escort and we caught her snoozing in the office, her rage knew no bounds! Ward sister, since she couldn't be rid of me, decided that I must be knocked into shape and I suffered considerably in the process.

When I heard on the grapevine that a new probationer was expected, I was much gratified. I should no longer be the lowest form of animal life. But when she arrived she was cute, curvaceous and came from Crewe. She had a boy-friend and a bicycle, and was able to cycle home on her evenings off, and she committed no foolish *faux pas*. I was consumed with envy.

June came in on a heatwave; patients shed their coverings and nurses their corsets. Lacking suspenders, we rolled our woollen stockings down to below the knee, securing them with bits of string and thereby inviting varicose veins in later years. Our long skirts hid the sacrilege.

The hospital was an open-air institution, but now we went a stage further and pulled the beds out on to the verandah for a limited time. Twenty minutes on the first day (it hardly seemed worth the bother), and a little longer on each succeeding day, until eventually the patients lay exposed to sunlight all day long. Much later, when lectures commenced, I was to learn that this method of sunning was the brain-child of a certain Dr Peabody; all our treatments were modelled on the lines advocated by Dr Peabody and Dame Agnes Hunt, an admirable lady of high repute and a friend of our senior surgeon.

For decency's sake the patients wore 'tidies', which were small rectangular pieces worn fig-leaf fashion and secured by tapes at each corner, like the lower half of a bikini, only less so. On the women's wards they were also permitted the dignity of a shapeless sort of brassiere and the elderly patients were allowed to go their own way, but there was no false modesty; only during visiting hours did adult patients don more concealing wear. This long exposure to sunlight is not now approved of, but certainly with the graduated method people acquired an enviable tan and no one ever suffered from sunburn.

It was my special responsibility, allied with bottles and bedpans, to see that the boys' tidies were clean and *in situ*. I was still disconcerted by this bit of male anatomy and never knew what to call it. The boys had no such problem and enjoyed my confusion. If I had to refer to it, it was the 'thing'.

I had so far escaped our senior surgeon, a non-resident commonly known as 'T'ogre'. T'ogre was reputed to arrive unheralded and strike like lightening, leaving the equivalent destruction in his wake. Sisters had hysterics, patients wept, student nurses went home to mother and even Nurse Jennings had been known to miss her lunch. Sister herself gave me the drill so that there could be no mistake; if ever the great man arrived when I was on duty, I was to make myself scarce. I could phone all the other wards to apprise them of his presence, but then I was to shut myself in the sluice until I was told it was safe to come out. I needed no second bidding.

One hot afternoon I laboured alone with the bedpans.

Sister was off-duty, the other nurses had gone to first tea, and staff nurse had disappeared on some secret mission of her own. A low warning whistle from the boys alerted me and I looked up to see a shining limousine glide to a halt at the steps leading to the ward. A short, stocky, florid-faced man alighted and scaled the steps with unlikely speed, and with horror I knew it must be T'ogre.

'I'll do the round!' he boomed. I made to escape, bleating something about staff nurse, but he had me by the arm.

'You'll do!' he barked, pushing me before him.

At each bed he paused, testing extensions, flexing groin-straps, sniffing at plasters, and his comments were caustic.

We came to a boy who for some reason was not so brown as the others. T'ogre pointed at him accusingly.

'Has that boy had his Peabody sunning?' he demanded.

I stared open-mouthed and wrathfully he repeated the question. 'Has that boy had his Peabody sunning?'

Suddenly, a great light dawned. Of course, how simple! So that was what they called it!

'Oh no!' I replied a little reproachfully. 'He's been sunned everywhere else but he wore a tidy over his peabody.'

* * *

Matron abhorred smoking and forbade it amongst the probationers. I had long been an offender, for those of us who made the journey to school by train enlivened the tedious trip with de Reske Minors in a pale green oval tin, paid for with bus fares accumulated by trudging the two miles between school and the station. Scorning the conventional carriage seats, we lounged on the luggage racks puffing away like addicts in an opium den.

Seasonal travellers gave us a wide berth, and walking home from the station I sucked peppermints, lest Father, a non-smoker, should detect the odour. Sometimes he complained of it in my hair, but attributed it to fellow passengers and advised me to travel in a non-smoker.

Now that the habit was forbidden it became a must for all of us, but matron soon got wind of the wicked weed and tracked down offenders ruthlessly.

Burning buckets of tow after the bedpan round was the obnoxious job of the junior probationers, but it was eagerly sought after by the seniors as an opportunity for a smoking session in the stoke-hole.

The Hall boasted a flat roof surrounded by battlements; our quarters, previously the servants', were on the top floor and the row of six lavatories at the end of the corridor had skylights opening out on to the roof. Anyone needing the loo for a legitimate purpose was invariably foiled by a row of nurses solemnly standing on the seats with their heads through the skylights, puffing away with great concentration.

In summer, the flat roof was a favourite place for sunbathing off-duty. It was made accessible by means of a small winding stairway, and it was a ludicrous sight to see a row of heads protruding at roof level, all smoking away like decapitated human chimneys.

Many matrons may be female automatons, but ours was just and kind, and really had our welfare at heart. Anyone could take their problems to her. They might be reprimanded, but never condemned. She made a home of the hospital and many of the younger patients remembered no other. One tiny child was encased in plaster because her bones were so brittle they fractured at a touch; just by moving her arm she could break it. But she was a merry child and had known no other life, for she was only two weeks old when she was admitted. Last time I saw her, she was still there but grown into womanhood.

A beautiful boy of four with golden curls and a cherubic face hurtled round the wards, sure of a welcome everywhere. His legs ended just below the knee and his feet stuck out like a frogman's flippers; his short arms terminated in a thumb and forefinger. Dennis had an inquiring mind and was a favourite of night sister's. One morning as he sat on her lap playing with the bunch of safety-pins festooned to her ample bosom he asked, 'Does all ladies wear pin-cushions underneath their aprons?'

Neither of these children had ever been acknowledged or visited by any of their families, but we were their family and they grew up assured of affection. Most of the patients, however, had devoted relatives who mourned their long absence from home.

Many of the children were polio victims. Their flaccid limbs were encased in walking calipers and they managed to get around under their own steam. Everyone had something, diseased hips, spines and knees, congenital deformities, or maybe limbs missing altogether, yet no one saw themselves as abnormal; the abnormal ones were those who had nothing wrong!

During off-duty on fine days we took the children out with us, pushing spinal carriages down country lanes, wearing our long hooded cloaks lined with red. Matron only allowed us to wear uniform in the vicinity of the hospital, for she reminded us that we were still untrained and if called on to deal with an accident or emergency, we might do more harm than good. Many of us would have stayed on, probationers growing older, but matron was adamant. After the stipulated two years she ousted us like fledglings from the nest to do our general training. Only sisters and staff nurses were allowed to make a niche for themselves.

For a long time it seemed that I was general dogsbody on the boys' ward. They were an unruly lot and mischievous to the extreme. When they were at last bedded down and all the sisters went to supper, the staff would congregate in the linen room to feast off cornflakes laced with the top of the milk and egg and chips, hurriedly prepared in the kitchen. But as a junior pro I was despatched to the ward to keep 'cave' and to control the boys. Strangely enough I found this no problem once I took on the role of story-teller, and providing I kept going, the boys fiercely disciplined each other.

Every evening I would crouch on a stool in the centre of the darkening ward narrating an endless serial story made up as I went along. Each episode terminated with the supper

73

bell and was recommenced the following night. The hero was an ingenious polio boy known as Harry Stotle, whose cunning was such that he constantly outwitted staff nurses, sisters and visiting consultants. He was aided and abetted by a one-legged crony called Hopper. Hopper's remaining appendage was of such strength and resilience that he was able to leap incredible distances, always bearing Harry with him. The couple led a hazardous existence, but with Hopper's projectile limb and Harry's know-how, nothing was impossible!

Wallybags was the most colourful character in the whole establishment. She was an Irish nurse of indeterminate age with fine dark eyes and a caustic humour. I was flattered when she elected to accompany me home when our day off coincided, but Wally was a staunch royalist and it was the day on which the Duke of Kent was to make Princess Marina his Duchess. With all the world to choose from they had elected to honeymoon in Dudley, at Himley Hall! When her day off was unavoidably cancelled, Wally was inconsolable. 'Bejapers, now oi'll never see herself,' she keened. Ironically, I had no wish to see her, for, I was going through an anti-royalist patch. Anyway, I had little time to traipse around gawping at the nobility.

As usual, the women patients had given me a long list of shopping to do for them. Many of the articles were unobtainable locally, so I had to go into town after all.

The buses were full, so I had to walk, and when I got there I found the main road was blocked with sightseers lining the route of the royal procession. I tried to push my way through the mass but some of the crowd were very truculent. I lost a shoe, had my bunion trampled on, and my beret got pushed over one eye. Then a great swopson of a woman butted me on the nose and it began to bleed furiously. My handkerchief had been lost in the mêlée.

As the cavalcade of cars came into view, the crowd surged forward bearing me with it. Dishevelled and bloody, I stumbled forward, falling with the flat of my hands onto the bonnet of a slow-moving limousine – only a policeman tugging at my coat saved me from the sacred wheels. The inside of the car was illuminated, and as it passed I saw, like a flashlight photograph, two Olympian beings, beautiful beyond description. She wore a little pillbox hat and was attired in the Marina green which she so favoured. As the vehicle bore her away, she turned and gave me her sad, sweet, lopsided smile and I was her fan for life.

*   *   *

When at last I graduated to the theatre block, I felt I had really got somewhere. Close proximity with T'ogre was rather daunting, for he began to call me 'the long one' and took a disturbing interest in my bunion. Before operating, he always took a bath and donned clean white trousers, white singlet and long white boots. The overall gown, gloves, skull cap and mask were of course taken from a sterilized drum in the theatre itself, together with a pair of long Cheadle forceps. It became my responsibility to prepare his bath and see that his gear was airing on the radiator; also that a bottle of concentrated orange juice was at hand, together with a syphon of soda water. He never drank water, maintaining that it 'rotted the guts', and always diluted his fruit drink with soda water. It made a refreshing beverage, for operating theatres are hot and thirsty places, and normally it was kept under lock and key, otherwise pilferers filched the orange juice, sacriligiously adding water to hide the theft.

Fear of infection to the patient was always the bogey that dogged our heels. Antibiotics were still a thing of the future and scrupulous care in sterilization was taken; tetanus spores, we were told, could withstand anything less than twenty minutes boiling. It says well for the drill that during my two years there I remember no outbreak of infection, other than the inevitable childish ailments, and there were no deaths.

No credit due to me! On my first day in the theatre I had been filled with enthusiasm and watched avidly as T'ogre made expert slashes with his scalpel, meanwhile concocting

75

in my mind dramatic reports for my next epistle home. I could hear Mother boasting to the aunts, 'Our Edie's operating now!' Suddenly T'ogre recalled me. 'Mop!' he bellucked and I darted into the corridor to the broom cupboard and was back in a flash with a mop. Anonymous gowned figures barred my re-entrance, scandalized eyes condemned me. Through the porthole windows I could see another, mopping the great man's brow.

The first amputation that I witnessed was from an advantageous position: I was holding the leg which was to come off. It was a very large leg from a very large lady, and when it was finally severed it was suddenly all mine and I nearly overbalanced from the sheer weight of it. I was not quite sure what I should do next. Abruptly, both the leg and I seemed superfluous. Hesitantly, I addressed T'ogre. 'Have you finished with it, sir?'

'God Almighty, girl,' he bellowed. 'What the hell would I do with it? Stuff it?'

'Burn it, you fool!' hissed theatre sister from behind her mask. 'In the stoke-hole!'

I swung round with my arms very full of leg, scattering the theatre staff, and blundered through the swing doors. Once in the corridor, I paused for reflection. I must get something to wrap it in. Reverently, I laid it on the floor as though it was still endowed with feeling.

I have never been any good at doing up parcels and a leg is not the easiest of objects to package. I tried to camouflage it with a discarded old sheet but however I wrapped it up, it still looked like a leg in a sheet. I gave up, and changed my theatre get-up for the less glamorous overall which sister had given me for cleaning the theatre floor after operations.

When I set off with my gruesome cargo I had to make several detours to avoid meeting people. I felt like a body-snatcher and just as guilty. The stoke-hole of course was situated in the basement. It was darksome and gritty with coke; the furnace had been recently replenished and there was not much room left for the leg. Revealed in the half-light with its trappings off, the leg was huge and bloated, but it tapered into a tiny little foot, a dear little foot, no corns, no bunions and surely only size four? What a waste, I mourned, comparing it with my own great clodhoppers.

There is something very personal about a lady's leg. Surely it warranted some small obsequial rite? But the idea of the burial service being read over a leg (with the owner as chief mourner) was ludicrous even to me. Bracing myself, I thrust it thigh first into the aperture. Immediately the leg assumed an independent existence and resisted me stubbornly. Desperately, we fought together. I pushed it frenziedly, flexing the knee, but when I released my hold it kicked back at me, clouting me on the nose which, true to form, began to bleed. Finally, by taking an unfair advantage with a shovel, I subdued the thing and slammed home the door of the furnace, from where it spat and hissed evil incantations. The unfortunate lady who had nurtured it so long seemed much happier without her leg, but I was never able to look her in the eye again.

* * *

My second winter came and snow drifted into the wards. It settled on the mackintoshed beds and joyfully the children snowballed each other where they lay. All day long we renewed the hot-water bottles round them. There were to be shutters on the wards for the next winter, but I should not be there.

The storms worsened, the electricity failed as did the telephones, the roads were impassable to traffic and we were cut off from the rest of the world.

Each morning we got up to dress in the corridor round a solitary candle. Hairdressing was easy, since it was all pushed under our caps anyway. Night nurses were worse off, with long lonely nights and fading torch batteries. Thank goodness for gas cookers!

Food stocks got lower, patients were given priority, and when reduced to the unusual luxury of biscuits, we longed for bread. On the fading radio we heard that the king was sinking fast. Matron thought that the bread might have been left at the station as trains were probably getting through. We volunteered to go after duty and she chose the six hardiest of us. The few male members of staff were mostly recruited from ex-patients and were disabled in some way, so they were not to be told.

After a supper of sorts we set off, intrepid and warmly clad, and with large waterproof laundry bags slung over our shoulders in anticipation of bread. At first it was fun, but snowdrifts lay deep and treacherous and it was not easy to keep to the road. Clinging together, we floundered through them. Lightening flashes illuminated the sky as telegraph wires collapsed from the weight of snow.

'When beggars die,' I quoted, 'there are no comets seen, but the heavens themselves blaze forth the deaths of princes.'

It was past midnight when we reached the station, but the bread was there. The old porter made us hot cocoa and told us the king had just died.

On the way back we were sobered and heavy laden; our thoughts turned to the new king. By all accounts he was a bit of a lad. Only I had seen him. When he had opened the new Birmingham–Wolverhampton road our headmistress had been one of the chosen to dine at the reception given for him and we were given the honour of lining the route at an advantageous spot. Actually, I had been acutely disappointed; he looked small and a little bow-legged to me. Perhaps it was all that horse riding, or maybe the long wait had jaundiced my eye. Someone in the crowd had cried, 'Oh! look at him walking!' as though she had never imagined he would have the use of his appendages.

I embroidered the event for them and glamourized the new king. I did not mention the legs. Anyway, they would not show under all that ermine.

In a few days things began to improve, and soon we were in circulation again. On the day of the old king's funeral we congregated with the patients to listen to it on the old steam radio. The commentator, with dolorous intonation, painted a picture of the pomp, the plumes, the solemnity and the sadness. Sombrely his voice droned on.

'With bowed head, following the coffin, walks the new king, the Duke of York on his right.'

'What's 'e say?' piped up an old girl in the corner. 'The Duke o' York on 'is bike?'

*   *   *

Suddenly the winter was gone, spring bloomed in the hedgerows and we intensified our strolls, planning the future with no inkling of the dark war years ahead.

'Gather ye rosebuds while ye may' – time was certainly aflying. Too soon it was May again and my turn to try my wings. Now would come the real grind; these two years had been only a preliminary for things to come. The hospital at which I had chosen to train was in a south-east coastal town not far from Broadstairs where Hilda was teaching, for I had a longing to be near to her, but I was keeping that as a surprise. (She was getting married shortly and moving to Bournemouth, but she was keeping that as a surprise!)

Night sister had laid bets that I wouldn't stay the course but that alone was to stand me in good stead and to goad me on when the going was hard.

All who were off-duty accompanied me on my last walk to the station, chatter and hilarity hiding real feelings. Over twenty years later my daughter was to tread the same road and in fact serve under the same staff nurse. On the platform we clung together unashamedly, but the train was as impatient as ever and had no time for tears. As it sped on its way I hung out of the carriage window watching the small group diminish until they had disappeared from view.

I had gathered my rosebuds.

CHAPTER FIVE

— Probationer Nurse —

AFTER THE EASY-going, predictable routine of orthopaedics, general training was like a douche of cold water. The training in voluntary hospitals was considered to be superior to that of county council establishments and we were very proud of the fact. Our existence depended on the goodwill of the community and there was no better basis for this than a satisfied customer.

Annually, when eggs were most prolific, we had a day when the townsfolk each contributed one. It was our job to pickle them and they sustained us throughout the year. Another day was dedicated to donations of Seville oranges and we suffered biliously from much marmalade-making.

Off-duty we organized our own amateur theatrical society and put on plays and concerts for the patients and staff and anyone else who could get in. They always went down well for we sought to emphasize the ludicrous situations in which we often found ourselves.

For a hospital to be supported by voluntary contributions there had to be many ways of raising funds. One was the carnival, which was held at the height of summer and well patronized by holiday-makers. We designed and decorated our own vehicle and it was a coveted privilege to be chosen to ride on it in the parade.

Waste was a cardinal sin and to practise economy was a part of our training. Visitors brought food rather than flowers and it was customary after they had gone to inspect patients' lockers to ensure that what they had brought was suitable. Tea, sugar and butter were most acceptable and were handed into the kitchen, as were new laid eggs, but fruit and soft drinks were left on the locker.

Preliminary training schools were unknown and seniority was accorded to first comers. Thus I left my old hospital as senior probationer to become again the most junior. The nurse who preceded me by two weeks had come straight from school. She was delighted by her improved status and meticulously initiated me into my duties. I was fortunate that she was only too anxious to save me from the snares into which she herself had fallen. Others were less charitable; seniors automatically took priority in the dining room and sleeping quarters, and we 'mucky pro's' accepted scanty servings and tepid bath water as our due.

Once more I found myself frequenting the stoke-hole to dispose of human rejects. The aborted twins I could never forget.

The woman who conceived them was a regular. She would never divulge her method of procuring abortions but this time the evidence was there in the form of a crochet hook which had got stuck.

The babies were too premature to qualify for a burial service. (It was customary to place miscarried infants at the feet of some adult corpse and I often speculated on the consternation of maiden ladies confronted at the Last Trump with a new-born babe sharing their coffin!) The disposal of them was left to me and I carried them wrapped in newspaper like a bundle of fish and chips.

All stoke-holes are much the same and I sat amongst the dusty jumble of coke and shovels nursing the little rejects on my lap and watering them with tears. Lofty of brow but minutely developed, they were obviously male; delicate fingers curled like limp petals and on their tiny faces were expressions of primeval wisdom and resignation. As I consigned them to the red-hot embers I was their only mourner.

81

'Why you mugwump,' scoffed sister when I returned with red-rimmed eyes. 'You'll never make a nurse!'

* * *

There was no ban on smoking except in the wards and dining room; it was an accepted thing so the pleasure was gone and I never smoked again.

Once more it was the top floor that harboured the nursing staff and the domestic staff too. As junior probationer, I occupied a tiny room next to that of matron's maid Millie, a belligerent female who regaled her mistress with exaggerated accounts of my misdemeanours. My bed was so narrow that if I wanted to turn over I had to get out first and get in backwards, and even that was not easy since the springs so sagged that my posterior was in constant contact with the floor. Millie complained of my nocturnal creakings and it was almost a relief when I was relegated to night duty.

So many nurses went sick when on night duty that it was customary to keep on indefinitely anyone who did not; consequently I spent nine months of my first year's training on nights. There were no nights off-duty until the end of the stint, when we were awarded one for each month that we had done.

I was feeling apprehensive when I reported for duty on my first night. I was carrying a covered meal on a tray, for there was only one nurse to each ward and no time off before 8.30 the following morning. As I stood to attention at ward sister's desk while she read her report to me I felt very important, for tomorrow morning she would be reading mine. She added several last-minute instructions and said there was a pile of mending in the linen cupboard to help me pass the time. She made it sound like a favour.

When the day staff went to their supper at nine o'clock, I was left alone. No, not alone! Belatedly, I remembered the patients. Quickly I changed into the rubber pumps worn by all the night nurses and made a tour of the ward, settling everyone down for the night. The men were a cheery lot and made my job as easy as possible.

I was just finishing when I got wind of the house surgeon, whose approach was always heralded by the aura of macassar with which he strove to subdue his unruly thatch, and in consequence of which he was popularly known as Pong. I wondered idly what he was doing in the kitchen until I remembered my meal which I had not yet investigated. Urgently I tracked him down. He was notoriously hungry, and as I anticipated, he was foraging for food.

Fortunately my tray had been pushed out of sight and his search revealed only bread, margarine and cocoa (ward sisters shrewdly locked up their poisons and provisions and secreted the key about their person). Undaunted by the meagre fare, he toasted thick hunks of bread and made cocoa for both of us. Obviously he was used to fending for himself.

The other commodity which he craved was an audience to whom to laud the merits of his current girlfriend, and we all knew about her to our cost. According to Pong, she was delectably delicious and had good connections to boot.

To stake his claim to this paragon he had invested in an engagement ring and was now beset by demands for the instalments on it. As he was reimbursed with half-a-crown for every post-mortem he performed, he carried out as many as possible, ghoulishly waylaying relatives for permission. It was usually granted willingly, since they were mollified by his interest – it was in the cause of science, he assured them. Heart conditions was his speciality; he did not add that the heart was his own!

Unfortunately we had to attend these macabre functions to further our knowledge of anatomy and so, although we had never met his betrothed, she was highly unpopular with us all.

Having satisfied the inner man, he ambled off to bed and sweet dreams. Poor Pong! They were short-lived, for it was a night of many admissions and he had to deal with them all. A house surgeon's lot is not a happy one.

Almost immediately night sister arrived to do her round, peruse the report, and read me the riot act. I was, she reminded me severely, very junior to be entrusted with the male surgical ward; matron had only chosen me because of sickness amongst the senior nurses and because she had in mind my two years' orthopaedic experience and inevitable knowledge of night work. Dutifully I acceded to the honour conferred on me but it was, I knew a double-edged compliment, for no 'oomph' girl ever did night duty on a male ward! Matron in her wisdom penalized all her charmers to servitude on the female wards.

My ward was the one nearest to the private suites of the mighty and I was to find the proximity most undesirable. To start with matron, whose vacation began on the morrow with an early flight, requested a call at 5 a.m. together with a light breakfast. Since no one so menial as myself could approach her in déshabillé, the calling was night sister's lot, but preparation of the breakfast was mine and the responsibility hung heavily upon me.

I was dealing with my first admission when Millie, on her way to bed, arrived with the sacred breakfast tray. She kept bobbing up and down behind the screen with instructions that went in one ear and out of the other, so that finally she gave up and went away.

The new patient with whom I was dealing was a very aged, unidentified man who had been found wading out to sea. He had resisted his would-be rescuers and was obviously not responsible for his actions. He had evidence of past strength in his great gaunt frame, but examination revealed a monstrous growth, which he must have piteously secreted for a very long time. When I had cleaned him up, night sister came and we fixed him with a drip saline, a sort of inverted thermos flask filled with a solution of salt and glucose and suspended at the head of the bed. It was connected to the patient by a length of rubber tubing and the fluid was regulated to be given by slow drip.

The next admission was a road casualty who had lost a great deal of blood. A transfusion was imperative. We had a book containing the particulars of blood donors and by referring to this Pong was able to select a suitable candidate who was roused from from his bed by the police and brought to the hospital. The donor lay on a bed alongside the patient but screened from view, and the transfusion was, as always, given direct.

The night, which at nine o'clock had stretched interminably before me, now rushed ahead like an express train down a dark tunnel. I could not keep pace with it. Sister's injunctions jostled for precedence in my head. Soon it would be morning and the busiest time of all.

The first streaks of dawn paled the sky when I remembered my meal, and immediately I was ravenous. I uncovered the tray with gratification; haddock! Already lightly cooked, it made a tempting dish, and a fresh brown egg (no pickled one this) with which to crown it obviously awaited poaching. Crisp rolls teamed with pats of real butter completed the repast, together with a grapefruit so exquisitely crimped and pared it seemed a sin to eat it, but I did so without compunction. Bully for cook; she evidently realized night staff needed cossetting!

With renewed vigour I pursued my tasks and was laying out the medicine trolley, the 'Black Jack' and 'White Mary' beloved of all ward sisters, when the house phone shattered the peace. It was night sister reminding me that she would be along in a few minutes to collect matron's breakfast. Heavens! I had forgotten! For one awful moment I could not find her tray; it had been pushed away in the corner of the kitchen. What was it Millie had muttered? I wished now that I had listened to her.

I lifted the covers and was astounded to see a revolting heap of spaghetti, congealed like roundworms, on a plate. Fancy them giving matron grub like that and look at mine.

Cold water trickled down my spine.

I knew that I was looking at it.

When I went on duty the following night, all and sundry knew that I had scoffed matron's breakfast; the juniors commiserated, the seniors crowed (that'll take her down a peg or two!). I just hoped matron had a very short memory and a very long holiday. I had managed to evade her before she went.

Ward sister was very snarky; her mind was on other things. 'Your old man,' she said (she was always to refer to him as this, as though I had perversely sought him out in the highways and byways just to annoy her!), 'has been giving a lot of trouble.' He had recovered from his dip in the sea sufficiently to pull down his drip saline and make a mess all over her ward. 'Her nurses' (I was not 'hers' – I was night sister's) had had a very trying day, and now they had to put up bed boards to prevent him from getting out of bed. Everyone knew how she detested bed boards, they made her ward so untidy.

The old man had been identified as a Mr Clay and had no known relatives. His age was indeterminate, but he was certainly in his nineties. Further, to vexate sister, there had been numerous discharges and the equivalent admissions, all for operation on the following day and therefore still ambulant. It exasperated her to see menfolk littering the ward; she liked them in two neat rows lying to attention with eight inches of the top sheet turned down and the vents in the pillow cases all facing away from the door. The men kept ragged bits of string of the required length under their pillows and measured their bit of sheet before she did her round, bequeathing them when they went home to the newcomers. Not that she would ever give vent to her ire on patients, but they felt the whiplash of her tongue when she berated the nurses.

Five of the new cases had inguinal hernias. I must do their initial preparing for operation and 'woe betide if they're not clean shaven'. I did take umbrage at this, for I was already reputed to be the slickest, speediest shaver in the business. With T'ogre's high standard behind me, I could be little else; let there be so much as a five o'clock shadow on his site of operation and he bellowed for the offender to be brought before him. That was one way of learning. Still she ranted on, so that it was with great relief that I saw her finally go off duty and flopped down into her chair, only to shoot to attention again as she came darting back, having forgotten to tell me to 'do' the bandages and not to forget the mending

I had not done the night before.

'Doing' the bandages was a tedious chore. They were white cotton bandages of a quality that varied according to the current financial status of the hospital funds and they had to be washed, boiled, ironed and wound up with a little rolling machine. They were used repeatedly until they literally fell to pieces. I found them soaking in the sluice, and after a quick rub, put them on to boil. If I got them done in time, one of the patients could roll them for me in the morning. I would get someone else to make the swabs for the drums, as I always hated that job because the cotton wool went up my nose. Packing the drums was a must for night nurses; they had to be filled with clean dressings and ready for the porter when he came on duty. He took them to the sterilizing room where they were dealt with and returned in time for the day staff to do the morning dressings. There was never enough cotton wool, but we used to open the new rolls and spread them over the radiators before packing – the warmth made them increase to twice their bulk.

Mr Clay had been given medication but it had not taken much effect, and when I went into the ward he was rattling the boards which gave his bed a coffin-like appearance and making hoarse animal noises. I hoped he was not going to keep that up all night. The inguinal hernia patients, drawn together by a common ailment, had formed a little clique and were nattering like women; anyone would think it was a pub. I would soon put a stop to that. I would shave them all now! Some of sister's bad temper had rubbed off on me. I rushed down the ward with screens and the necessary equipment and got on with the job, anxious to finish before night sister put in an appearance. The hernias fell silent and eyed each other apprehensively.

I suppose to be so intimately attacked by a crazy teenage female with a cut-throat razor could be a little off-putting; they lay petrified and unresistant. I had shed all my false modesty in the past two years and worked with speed and precision. It was like a sheep shearing. Before night sister arrived, everything was cleared away and the ward lights dimmed; only a row of little humps under the bedclothes suggested my victims were anxiously investigating to see if I had done them a mischief.

The recipient of the previous night's transfusion was so improved that I did not recognize him until he greeted me like an old friend, but Daddy Clay was a thorn in the flesh. Pong wrote him up for further medication, but it was no more effective than the first; his carcinoma and incontinence were very offensive, and when I tried to clean and change him, he resisted violently and sought to cover the foul growth as though to him it was a shameful thing. I made some gruel and fed him from a spoon; he pursed his lips, supped it like a baby, and clung to me with a fierce grip lest I should go with it unfinished. After that he began a slow rhythmic motion as though his boarded bed was a boat he was rowing through a heavy sea. Once he ceased only to peer into the shadows like some pale ghost before cupping his hands to his mouth and letting out a long 'Halloo!' which pierced the night like a clarion call, startling all the men and rousing the assistant matron from her bed.

'Really, nurse!' she snapped. 'Can't you manage your ward better than this?'

I put a light over the old man's bed and the small ward table and chair beside it, and then I took my various chores and charts and did them beside him. Each time he raised his hands to repeat the hallooing I shushed him severely, but the patients were resigned to a sleepless night and tossed relentlessly. I felt sorry for the operation cases; they would be lying awake dreading their ordeal. It would soon be morning, and there was so much to remember. I must not forget their early morning specimens. All the pre-operative men must have their urine tested and it must be the first they passed in the morning.

I had begun the report when out of the corner of my eye I saw one of the hernias slip out of his bed and make for the toilet. My specimen! I dashed in after him. 'Wait! Please wait!' I cried urgently. 'I want a specimen from you.' He paused apprehensively, wondering what fresh indignity was to be committed on him.

'I want a specimen of your urine,' I explained patiently. He still looked nonplussed. A row of specimen glasses stood waiting up on the shelf and I pointed to them. 'I want you to pass water into one of those.'

'What!' he cried aghast. 'From 'ere!'

* . * . *

Daddy Clay clung tenaciously to his miserable life, to the great vexation of ward sister. He appeared to have outlived his contemporaries and no relatives came forward. Geriatric institutions would have accepted him but not his malignant tumour, and as soon as the side ward became empty, sister had him moved in there. At least her ward was tidier without him, though it had the disadvantage of bringing him within range of her office. She complained bitterly of the obnoxious effluvia and burned foul-smelling cones to eradicate it; of the two I preferred Daddy Clay. He still kept up his strange hallooing and indefatigably rowed his boarded bed. Drugs had little effect on him, and his hoarse cried could be heard all over the hospital. 'Old Stinker' was decried by all. The night staff's quarters were situated just above the ward and intermingled with the clatter of bedpans and the cag-mag of visitors, his halloos haunted us all day; not that we could sleep in any case. The staff linen room was at the end of our corridor and the assistant matron was constantly toing-and-froing and rustling laundry paper. Also, we were roused to attend lectures, and Millie, who came to call us, plodding along on her great flat feet, usually woke the wrong people anyway!

The holiday season was in full swing bringing with it the usual spate of casualties, and the pier more than anything else contributed to these. There was the man who dived off it into two feet of sea and broke his neck; another, tempted by the 'try your strength' contraption, fractured his spine; and then there was the boy who was doing nothing in particular except watching the fishermen and got a fish hook in his face. Fish hooks were a common casualty in Out-Patients and were easily removed by simply cutting off the line and pushing the hook itself through, like a sewing needle, to a different point of exit. The boy's father, however, had persistently tried to pull out the hook from the point of entrance, causing severe laceration resulting in infection. The boy was now critically ill with cellulitis of the face. The cruel barb, of course, prevents the hook from being pulled back. Poor dumb fish. Their very silence condemns them; if only they could give voice to their agonies there would be fewer fishermen!

*   *   *

I had just settled the ward patients for the night and had prepared the leeches in a shallow receiver when the phone rang in sister's office. Even then leeches were somewhat antedeluvian, but they were useful for the local abstraction of blood and were much favoured by our old eye surgeon for the relief of congestion. It was quite customary for his patients to be sporting three in a row above the eyebrow. After about an hour, each having taken about three teaspoonfuls of blood, they would drop off, sleepy and happily replete. They were more trouble to put on, being somewhat temperamental; trust sister to leave the job for me! Any perfume or disinfectant was guaranteed to put them off, so that the prospective patient had to be cleansed with plain water and the area in question left moist and then covered with white lint in which holes had been cut to allow the leech to bite.

Leeches do not like being handled either, so it was necessary to almost fill a test tube with cotton wool, slip in the leech, broad end downwards and then tilt the tube so that the suckers made contact with the skin. Even then they were sometimes reticent and needed coaxing by smearing the patient's skin with a little sweetened milk, but once they had the right idea they hung on like grim death. As they produced a substance which prevented the clotting of blood, the bleeding often continued after they had fallen off

Top: Standon Hall, rear view
Above: 'Peabody sunning!'
Left: After the 'All clear'

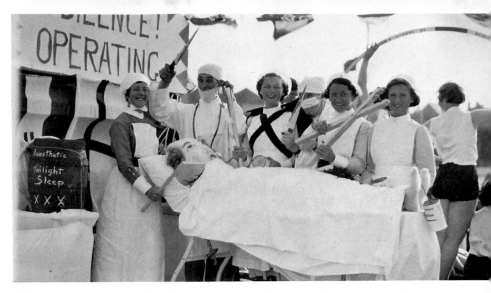

Above: Margate General and District Hospital's entry for the carnival, 1939. We tran[s]formed our vehicle into a mock-operating theatre, the patient being constructed fro[m] pillows and artificial limbs. As we swayed through the streets, the two men, decked o[ut] in surgeon's garb, withdrew endless coils of rubber tubing from its abdomen, to t[he] ghoulish joy of the crowd. *Left to right:* Out-Patient Sister, 'Gur', Self, 'Pong', Nur[se] Cameron and 'The Babe'. *Below left:* Gunlayer's rescue, 1939 *Below right:* The phot[o]graph 'The Babe' carried with her

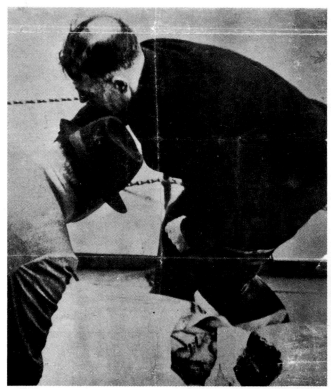

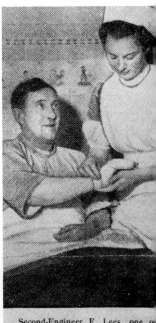

Second-Engineer F. Lees, one o[f] the four survivors of the Aberdee[n] steamer Rubislaw which struck a min[e] off the South-East coast on Tuesday[,] in hospital. Thirteen members of th[e] crew were lost, the four being picke[d] up by a minesweeper.

satiated and sometimes it was necessary to apply a styptic to the triangular bite mark which was left. Some hospitals used their leeches only once and then destroyed them, but we dropped ours into a jar of strong salt solution so that they obligingly vomited and could be used again. Dracula in particular was a lusty leech, lighter in pigmentation than his companions and very active. Sister was quite fond of Dracula.

When the phone rang so inopportunely, I put the leeches down on sister's desk while I answered it. Dracula was impatient for his feed and made several attempts to escape, so that I had to keep pushing him back with my finger. Then, to delay me further, Pong appeared, but I had good news for him. A patient who had been discharged that afternoon kept a local winkles and welkes stall with jellied eels to boot, and he had left Pong a large brown paper bag of his wares, shelled and ready for consumption. Pong was delighted with his windfall and hurried into the kitchen in search of vinegar. The bag had been waiting on the desk for a considerable time and had become rather moist, so that when he picked it up the bottom fell out, scattering the contents all over the desk, but he was by no means fussy and went back to the kitchen for a basin and swept them all in.

Then, established in sister's chair and with his feet on her desk, he settled down to enjoy his treat, and even the arrival of night sister did not disturb him. She viewed him with disfavour. Really! The way that young man bolted his food! A potential gastric ulcer if ever she saw one! She read the report and then, looking round for something to complain of, saw the receiver. 'Sister's desk,' she said severely 'is no place for that sort of thing!' Actually, she was looking at Pong's boots, but I picked up the receiver to mollify her.

Dracula! He was gone! He must have escaped during the kefuffle; no sign of him on the desk either. I gazed in horrid fascination at Pong as he put down his empty basin and smacked his chops in appreciation; then he belched deeply with great satisfaction and began picking his teeth with the trocar which he kept in his pocket for that purpose. Night sister could stand it no longer. 'Disgusting man!' she snorted, and swept out like a brig in full sail.

'*Virgo intacta*!' muttered Pong in retaliation as he ambled out after her. I searched every place but I never did find Dracula and his disappearance was one more thing for ward sister to hold against me.

* * *

I still continued to feed Daddy Clay his bowl of gruel at night, and on catching sight of me he would begin to mouth in anticipation. I hoped ward sister would not find out, but before long she was complaining that I used more than my quota of milk. After that I began getting tins of baby food and sneaking them in under the scarlet cape with which all night nurses were provided. One night, for the first time, he rejected it. He had given up his rowing too, and kept heaving his long bony legs over the bed boards in an effort to escape. Towards the dawn there was an obvious deterioration in his condition. I tried to remember when it was high water, for they invariably went out with the tide. If he died before eight o'clock I would have to lay him out, but if he lasted until then it would be the day staff's job. Towards eight when I went in to feel his pulse he gripped my hand, but his hoary eyes stared right through me and saw me not at all. Feebly he tried a last 'halloo', but in the middle of it his mouth fell slackly to one side and he was gone. Staff nurse, who had just come on duty, stood in the doorway, looking closely at her watch. 'He's all yours,' she said, and hurried away so that she would be the first to tell sister.

We were not allowed to perform 'last offices' until at least one hour after death. 'A mark of respect' they said, but it also gave time for the process of elimination to be completed; so I would have to come back after 'supper' (night staff meals were all back to front!). When she read the report, ward sister was almost cheerful. One day she would smile by mistake and never forgive herself!

When I returned, Stinker's face had settled into that benign expression which so often follows death, and he looked surprisingly young and quite handsome. After I had finished I was very pleased with the result; unloved and unlamented, he lay with the dignity of a patriarch.

The following evening the ward seemed strangely subdued. As usual one of the men had saved the local paper for me and it lay spread out on the kitchen table. From the front page a familiar face stared up at me, a youthful Clay, bold and stalwart in sou'wester and life jacket.

'Tribute to our Sailor Son!' screamed the headlines.

'Lifeboat coxswain for forty years!'

They had dug deep into their archives; his seamanship was phenomenal, his exploits legion. Countless lives had been saved by his incredible courage and strength, and his refusal to admit defeat. A civic funeral was to be arranged for the hero.

I had many lessons yet to learn, but 'Old Stinker' had taught me the most important one of all.

*   *   *

At last I came off night-duty bewitched, bothered and bewildered, and a confirmed insomniac. The world had suddenly stopped and was now going the wrong way round. I had four days off, or was it nights?, in which to get rehabilitated, and I spent them with Hilda who was now married and living in Bournemouth.

When I returned to hospital I was back with my own age group: 'Torti' Collis, 'Pansy' Plant, 'Moke' and 'Gentle Jane', who had certainly never been christened Jane and who had tried so hard to buffer me from the hard knocks when I first came. We had all attained status during the past year and I had now been allocated to Out-Patients.

My first morning there was a revelation concerning the things people did to themselves and to one another! And the places they got things stuck in, and the things they got stuck in the places! No wonder sister was a spinster; it was enough to put anybody off. But she was very jolly and a joy to work with. It was her half-day, but as she said there was nothing much doing in the afternoon, only the psychiatric clinic and that was nothing – only you had to stand no nonsense from the patients and have all the files ready and in order for Dr Hatter, the psychiatrist, who was very particular about having all the files ready and the patients lined up correctly. Any fool could do that.

The patients began to arrive far too early; obviously they enjoyed their psychiatric sessions with Dr Hatter. I took their particulars and sat them down on the benches in the right order, but they would keep jumping up and changing their seats and behaving like unruly children. One was a real upstart and just would not be still. He was a little cartoon-like character with a too-long coat, a bowler hat and thick pebble glasses. He would keep bobbing up and down. I got quite cross and took him by the hand and led him to the end of the back bench. He could jolly well wait till last. 'Sit there,' I said, giving him a little push, and he sat. 'Now, what name did you say it was?'

'Hatter,' he said.

*　　*　　*

Whenever possible we participated in the local sports displays. Matron was all for good healthy sport. I was, too; I reckoned to provide for my Christmas and birthday gifts with the proceeds. I once gave a fine ten-day clock as a wedding present, the recipients being dazzled by its munificence until they took it from the box to reveal a card: '1st Prize, 200 yds.'

Most of the sports were held at Canterbury, where the nurses had a sports ground and a huge new white hospital of which they were inordinately proud. There was much rivalry between us. In our own humble way we also had a sports club which we supported ourselves by self-appointed duties. Pansy pleated uniform caps at a ha'penny each, Moke polished shoes, I plucked eyebrows – a penny each – and wrote rude rhymes to order. We even dug and delved a small allotment, granted by the grace and favour of matron, and sold the produce to cook. The soil was very mediocre and once, in the dark hours of the night, we crept out in our oldest clobber and robbed a neighbouring farmer of his manure heap. He was furious when he discovered the loss, but never thought to seek it at the hospital next door.

Eventually our hard-earned pennies so increased the club funds that we were able to afford a tennis court. It was a proud achievement and we urgently wrote home for the old rackets which we had wielded at school.

Finding the time to play was another matter, for lectures were all held in our off-duty time, and then they had to be written up in exercise books to be used for swotting at some later date. Even so, the courts were usually occupied on fine evenings after supper, and patients in the wards which overlooked them leaned out of the windows shouting encouragement and advice until night sister doing her rounds shushed them all back to bed.

Hospital exams were of paramount importance, for until they were satisfactorily passed one was not allowed to enter for the all-important state examinations. At last after two years of endless chores and interminable lectures, and with our hospital exams behind us, we were qualified to take our preliminary state examination. It was a momentous occasion, but costly. Since our training was at a voluntary hospital, we had to fork out the two pounds entrance fee ourselves. Our salaries were fifteen pounds in the first year, twenty pounds the second year, and twenty-five pounds the third year, but from that was deducted insurance money and money for uniform and study books. Ward sisters, superior beings, actually earned fifty pounds per annum!

In addition to the entrance fee there was our fare to London, where the ordeal was to take place at St Stephen's Hospital. As usual Father turned up trumps, but we had to have a whip-round for Moke.

We each had a chart listing the accomplishments with which we should be familiar and each attainment had to be initialled by a sister verifying our proficiency. Sisters were very chary, however, of signing these documents lest we should, at some later date, prove inefficient and it be traced back to them. In any case, they always insisted on seeing the chore performed again before their very eyes, and were cross with us for asking because they really hadn't got the time.

Consequently some of us had charts up to date, but the railway carriage in which we travelled was very crowded so we passed them round and got them initialled that way. It looked quite authentic and everyone was delighted to oblige.

Our fellow travellers were a jolly lot; they even took part in our last desperate swotting session, joining happily in the jingles we employed to refresh our memories.

First the symptoms of syphilis:
There was a young man of Bombay,
Who thought chancres would soon fade away,
Until he got tabes
And gummatas babies
And thought he was Queen of the May.

We were a bit weak, too, on the bones of the wrist, but Torti, who had recently fractured hers, was well up on this:

Scaphoid
Semilunar
Cuneiform
Pisiform
Trapezium
Trapezoid
Os Magnum
Unciform.

'Slowly Sailing Cooking Peas Travelling Towards My Ulna,' we chanted, and when we reached the Great Metropolis our fellow passengers went off to their humdrum office jobs muttering, 'Slowly Sailing Cooking Peas . . .'

It took us some time to track down St Stephen's Hospital, but once there we found large arrows directing entrants to the examination room. Our high spirits were sadly depleted now; most of all we dreaded the compulsory question, and when the papers were handed round we covertly rolled our eyes at each other. The enforcing question was: 'Give the life history of a bug.'

Heading our primary paper was a space in which to record any disability from which we might be suffering and, which might detract from our performance.

Moke was just recovering from hepatitis, and Torti still had her wrist in plaster. It was her left, but sister had told her she might mention it for consideration. I felt peeved that they should both have such unfair advantages over me, and just before the papers were collected I scribbled in my vacant space 'Born in an air raid.'

The practical part of the examination took place in the afternoon after a lunch of dubious mince and rice pudding. We stood for hours in a long dark corridor at the top of the building and a lift went constantly up and down creating an infernal draught.

We were blue with cold when a woman like a praying mantis stuck her head out from a nearby doorway and called, 'Nurse Collis!' Torti, with a grimace, followed her in.

We were to go in alphabetical order and poor Pansy by the time they got to her was cyanosed and dithering with the cold. The first task allotted to her was to fill an ice bag, and she had to start from scratch with a small pick and a large lump of ice.

When my turn came I was ushered into a room in which tables were heaped with all sorts of hospital equipment; obviously my predecessors had all had a good rummage through it. At another table sat the examiners, and genuine hospital patients sat or lay in beds, waiting to be performed on and looking as though they were having a whale of a time.

The first job I got was to apply a mustard plaster, so I gazed at the jumble on the tables and wondered where to start. One of the examiners who looked vaguely familiar leaned forward. 'You'd better get this right,' he said. 'I think

I signed for it.' I stared unbelievingly at him, and softly he began to chant, 'Slowly Sailing Cooking Peas . . .'

In spite of everything we passed, and proudly wore white chevrons on our sleeves to substantiate the fact. Now we were really on the way up. Matron gave me the job of senior nurse on the women's surgical ward and, elated, I scrutinized my features in the mildewed mirror of my bedroom. Perhaps I was going to be a swan after all!

There had always been 'Trouble in the Balkans', but suddenly the Balkans were a lot nearer; refugees were coming over in droves, camps were set up for them and some, for reasons of health, were admitted to hospital. In their halting speech they told terrible tales of torture and pleaded piteously for money to bring over their aged Yiddisha mommas, refusing to believe that we had none or that our parents would not be forthcoming if approached. On the back of the office door Pong pinned a picture. It depicted a small mongrel dog gazing ecstatically at a large poster which bore the legend: '10,000 Poles for Britain.'

Matron gave hospital room to some refugee nurses and we tried to help them improve their limited knowledge of our language, but their methods of nursing were so alien and they were very critical of ours. To our amazement they insisted on taking to their beds during menstruation (fancy even letting anyone know!). They said it was customary in their native land, but we did not believe it.

We had a new student and were forewarned that she was very young, just seventeen, and straight from school. Matron was taking her to oblige her father, but she would not officially begin her training until she was eighteen, the stipulated age. When she arrived, she was loose-limbed and coltish, with huge brown eyes fringed with black 'sweep's brush' lashes. They were her only claim to beauty, but when she had learned how to use them she would need nothing else. She was so young it broke your heart, and it was a crying shame to turn her loose amongst us.

She had spent most of her life in kindergartens and boarding schools, but she had a father who was a very dashing lieutenant-commander in the Royal Navy. When he was on leave they had a proper 'beano'. Somewhere there was a twin sister and a mother, but her parents had been divorced and her mother had custody of one twin and her father of the other. We thought the dashing father sounded interesting and inquired when the next beano was due, but he had only recently rejoined his ship. Just our luck!

That first night after 'lights out' she came scuttling into my room afraid of the dark. I was incredulous and reprimanded her sternly; if she told anyone else she was for it. I had once admitted to a fear of spiders and ever since my bed had been a dumping ground for them. She was accustomed to sleeping in dormitories where a dimmed light was kept for convenience, so I saw her back to her own room and left her the torch with which I had been reading under the bedclothes. After that I had a feeling that she spent all her pin money on batteries. She seemed to see in me the mother for whom she had been searching, and I just could not get her off my back. In vain I told her it was not done for seniors to fraternize with juniors. She dubbed me a 'stuffy old fuddy-duddy', and was not a whit abashed. Everywhere she dropped clangers, and we were very careful what we gave her to do. Delegated to help the vicar with his communions, she knocked over his improvised alter and came out with a four-letter word which was never let loose outside the common-room (not the one you're thinking of either, but far, far worse!). Of course she did not know the meaning, but the dear man was so shocked that he obviously did.

When instructed to clean the loo with soda water our young student was found squirting our one precious syphon down the S-bend, and when told to deliver a patient in her wheelchair to the X-ray department, she managed to squeeze the patient, the wheelchair and herself into the food lift so that they all ended up in the basement kitchen. Cook, who was expecting the joint, dissolved into hysteria and it took the combined efforts of all the kitchen staff half an hour to release them from the lift, only to find that there was no other way out of the kitchen which had not been built to accommodate wheelchairs. The patient, now inclined to hysteria as well, refused to be sent up alone, so it took them all just as long to pack the intruders back into the lift in order to be rid of them. Dinner was very late that day.

The 'Babe', as she was now known, was so anxious to learn and to redeem herself that I taught her how to test the urines. Dejectedly she registered 'NAD' (nothing abnormal discovered), and longed to find something really exciting. One evening, when we were all rushed off our feet but had nothing we dared to give her to do, she decided she would test the urine of all the staff; after all, you never know what you might find there! Poor Babe, I was afraid she would be disappointed. We all obliged her with a specimen, but I surreptitiously added a large tablespoonful of glucose to mine. After that we were so hectic I thought no more of it.

When we came from supper and made our way to our own quarters, Pong was waiting at the stairway. 'A word in your ear, wench,' he murmured, taking me by the elbow and manoeuvring me into his own doorway. He indicated a chair and by his solemn demeanour I knew that there was something much amiss. My heart missed a beat; it must be something very terrible that I had done. 'I'm afraid,' he said without preamble, 'that it's possible you may be a diabetic.'

I had completely forgotten the urine testing, but relief flooded over me deliciously. I had not killed anybody after all! I felt a right gawby, however, when he went on to explain how a tearful Babe had taken my specimen to him and begged him to save me, and it was even worse having to account to her. She quite forgot her previous concern for me and thought only of how I had fooled her. 'I'll never forgive you! Never!' she wept, and the juniors stood aghast to hear a senior so addressed.

She soon forgot not to forgive me and was busy vilifying Pong, who persisted in calling her 'sweet pea'. Despite ourselves, she brought a youthful optimism to our ranks. She also brought the mumps, and one by one the staff succumbed. Practically no one had had it and those who had, only on the one side. Now they had it on the other.

I was due for annual leave but of course it was postponed. I had never caught mumps myself; my early escapade with the night soil appeared to have immunized me against everything. It was very disheartening. Soon I was the most junior nurse left. In spite of my chevrons I 'ran' between wards doing bedpans and the most menial tasks while sister and staff nurses held the fort in other directions; even matron and the ass. mat. pithered around soothing the fevered brows and getting under everybody's feet.

Then it was Sunday, my 21st birthday. No post, no greetings; just one long bedpan round. From the sick bay came the sound of Torti's record player and much merriment; the sufferers were making the most of their convalescence. Oh well, one good thing came out of it: at twenty-one I was old enough to take my State Final.

CHAPTER SIX

— Gun-layer —

I WAS WORKING in the theatre when I heard war declared, the operating surgeon having brought in a portable wireless, thereby creating a precedent. The patient, a Czech refugee, was for Ceasarean section, and the child was being delivered through her abdominal wall as the fatal words were spoken. Almost immediately the sirens began to wail. We all eyed each other and wondered where we had left our gas-masks. It was generally believed that gas warfare was imminent and everyone had been warned to be always prepared, but very soon the all-clear sounded. It had only been an unidentified plane bringing, it was rumoured, the Duke of Windsor.

For a time everything remained quiet and it was all a bit of an anti-climax. But not for long. Insidiously a magnetic mine belt had been laid around our part of the coast, and with ceaseless repetition ships were blown out of the water. Usually a distant boom rattled all the windows and sent us scurrying to prepare beds and fix up drip salines for the survivors. Sometimes there were no survivors at all; and, after the golden summer, winter had come early with a biting cold, and many of the shipwrecked perished before the lifeboats could reach them.

I was put in charge of the children's ward, though answerable to sister on the nearby women's ward. It had been cleared of children, except for the side wards, and had been filled to capacity with government beds: horrid contraptions that folded up the middle, usually when you least wanted them to.

One of the first ships to be wrecked was the *Mastiff*, ironically a minesweeper. The four survivors were in the sea for five hours before being picked up, and the sea was frozen for the first time in living memory.

'What have we got this time?' I asked the junior who was escorting them up from casualty.

'Three whites and a lascar,' she replied, and the lascar sat up spluttering, to reveal himself to be the chief engineer covered in oil. Of the others, one was so severely and extensively burned that the newspapers had already reported him dead; another had the most appalling head injuries, yet incredibly was conscious and lucid, and had been pleading with the lifeboatmen to be thrown back into the sea. The last had a battered face and two fractures of the skull, but he looked as though he might make it. The first head injury we mercifully kept under morphine until he died. Later two women, wan after an interminable journey, arrived to see him. I had to go down to the mortuary to renew his dressing before I dared take them. They were his mother and fiancée, and they were past tears.

For one terrible fortnight not a day or night passed without at least one ship falling foul of the mines. Government beds extended into the corridors and every available space, and a full night's sleep was something which had only happened in the dim past. Townsfolk, too, with one accord turned out to help with the rescue work; all suitable vehicles helped supplement the ambulance services and seaworthy boats helped the overworked lifeboats.

One night, roused by night sister, we trundled wearily downstairs to find the large entrance hall choc-a-bloc with hysterical lascars, over forty in all. They had just been rescued from the sea and were slimy with oil, and not one spoke any English. Simultaneously the town's electricity supply was cut. Hours passed before it was restored and the ensuing chaos was indescribable, as with foraged torches we sorted the living from the dead, the badly injured from the not so bad, the not so bad from the uninjured. The latter were the ones making the most noise and they were taken in by local hoteliers.

The most badly injured were with us for a very long time; there was Ali-Ram-Jam and Ali-Ram Hasi (they were all Alis), and they would happily have stayed with us for ever. The other patients taught them a jargon of English and they had only to see anyone in a white coat or even slightly resembling a doctor, to sit up in bed rubbing their bellies and wailing 'Plenty much pain backside!'

Slowly the navy got the uppermost of the mine belt and wrecks became less frequent, and then the town echoed with the tramp of boots and the trundle of heavy vehicles as the army paused briefly en route for Dover and embarkation. During their respite a virulent attack of food poisoning decimated their ranks (many hinted at germ warfare), and our government beds were commandeered for soldiers. The senior service was very resentful; it was their billet and they wanted us to have no truck with the army, and the army, knowing what sailors are, cautioned us against them.

One night, going off-duty, I called for Pansy on the way and found her in despair. 'I've got a right lot in now,' she cried. 'They're supposed to be British but they can't speak a word of English.' Perhaps they were fifth columnists, I thought, and curious to see these phenomena I followed her into the ward where a motley crew sat up in their beds. One still had his cap on. They all stared at me and the hatted one called out: 'Yoh 'ave a goo at thissun, Bill. 'Er doh luk so sawney as t'other beesum. Goo on yer blether-yed. Aks 'er afore yoh bost!'

Bill looked at me miserably, but without hope. 'Wheer's the double yew, nus?' he pleaded. 'I wanta cack.'

Grudgingly ward sister allowed me to visit the Black-country crew during my free time to get them sorted out, but she was very hostile for they tried her sorely. She considered I was of the same ilk and once more, in her illogical way, attributed them to me. Poor sister! The government beds alone had a traumatic effect upon her tidy mind. They were elongated and angular, and stuck out like sore fingers. Worse still, instead of two neat rows like soldiers on parade, she had to have a row down the middle of her ward as well; it was always getting pushed out of line, and her lovely aspidistra, which had taken pride of place for so long, had been banished to the sluice. It had been the unenviable lot of the junior probationer to tend the monster and polish its massive leaves daily with olive oil, but now, abused and out of sight, it became the butt for everyone's spite when they fell foul of sister's spleen.

I was always sure of a warm welcome from my compatriots and we enjoyed a good dialectical argy-bargy, to the mystification of the other members of the ward. They were soon up and about and one day I was surprised to find them all missing except Sandy Banks. Sandy sought to explain their absence with decorum: 'It's ockard like,' he bawked, scratching his close-cropped ginger poll (sister had confiscated his cap). 'They aye 'ere 'cos they aye bin – but they've 'ad summat wot'll mek 'em goo – so when they've bin they'll cum.'

Later we took chairs and clustered round the coal fire at the end of the ward where it was cosier, but they cried out in alarm when sister, collecting clients for the padre, paused pen in hand and demanded, 'Any of you want communion in the morning?'

'We doh want nought,' bellucked Slasher Perry. 'Why we bin sot on the bog till we nigh on took root.'

'What exactly did he say?' sister asked of me coldly. 'He said, 'No thank you sister,' I replied, and she stalked off unbelieving.

'Why the franzy ines,' chuntered Charlie Peace. ''Er needn't come 'ere with 'er arse in 'er 'ond.'

In quieter moments we reminisced nostalgically about the Clent Hills and Kinver Edge and mourned sadly for the lost beauty of Baggeridge Woods which they told me were condemned to the axe, but soon they too were gone, swept up by the evil machinations of war.

Pong also had deserted us to become a ship's doctor. The

new houseman was brilliant at surgery and the art of seduction, and to aid his philandering he had a little tin lizzie. Her doors were tied together with bits of string and anyone tempted aboard with amorous intent usually had their ardour cooled by having to help push her back. We were amused by his Casanova capers and dubbed him Cass for short.

Ships continued to go down but less frequently; the latest was a French vessel and her crew, not too badly injured, were cheekily charming and wholly delightful. Enchanted by our schoolroom French they had no difficulty in making themselves understood.

'Darling, je vous aime beaucoup.
Je ne sais pas what to do . . .'

The *Mastiff*'s burned stoker and fractured gun-layer, who had been banished to a side ward, scowled and glowered, developing unspecified symptoms to draw attention to themselves.

They were our oldest inhabitants and took on proprietary rights. Now ambulant, they had become efficient at relieving us of fundamental chores and sought to make themselves indispensable. They would have been transferred to a naval hospital long since had not those establishments been full to overflowing. Cass was most anxious to be rid of them and schemed to hoof them out, but we fooled him by keeping bandages on their injuries for longer than was necessary. Matron turned a blind eye to our subterfuge; she disapproved strongly of Cass and obstructed his every move on principle. Also, the Royal Navy coughed up £2 for daily maintenance, which was corn in Egypt!

The rehearsals for our traditional Christmas concert were in full swing when it was decided that the State Final examination, postponed at the outbreak of war, should now take place at Canterbury instead of London. Lectures and studies had been at a standstill for so long that the ass. mat., whose duties extended to that of sister tutor, doubted we would make it, except perhaps for the knowledgeable

Torti – Pansy, Moke and myself had always been laggards. We thought bitterly of the days when you could buy your SRN and speculated on how many of our superiors might have come by it that way. The ass. mat. kept hinting that with finals looming imminent I should forgo my part in the concert this year. I would sooner have given up finals. Besides, I had composed a rhyme incorporating all the senior staff and ridiculing their peculiar foibles. It was rather impertinent, but wedded to a popular tune and performed by Babe, who could get away with anything, it would be a riot. Babe was delighted with her performance and wondered if perhaps she was depriving the world of a great artiste by taking up the mundane job of nursing.

The day before our examination, matron gave us finalists the day off. The others decided to spend it swotting, but last-minute cramming had never done anything for me and I decided to spend it with my friend Gina. Although severely disabled with arthritis, Gina lived alone and her incapacities were compensated by a dry wit and a nimble mind. On fine days, with my help, she would make it to the shore where she loved to be, and we would watch fascinated as planes equipped at the base with a huge metal ring skimmed the sea and thus attracted to the surface magnetic mines which they promptly machine-gunned. Since the weather had deteriorated, however, we had begun to decorate her little flat and this day off was a welcome bonus. Inevitably it began with a lie in, for I knew that when the others came up to make their beds after breakfast, someone would bring me a tray of tea and toast and marmalade. It was something we always did for each other.

This time it was the faithful Babe, who was wild with excitement as she plonked down my tray with a clatter and flung herself on to the bed, her arms round my neck. Really, would she never learn to show respect! She had just received a letter from her wonderful, wonderful father, who would be on leave in a few days so that another beano was due. Unable to control herself, she rolled about my bed like a young puppy.

Sternly I took her to task and reminded her that tomorrow I was taking my State Final! Immediately her mood changed and she sat up in consternation. 'Oh,' she wailed, 'I haven't got your mascot yet and I'm not off till this evening and the shops'll be closed!' (It was usual for potential examinees to be given mascots by their friends.) Then with mercurial charm she brightened. 'Silly old mascots. I'll do something practical instead. I'll get your uniform ready, sew on the buttons and everything.'

Now that was something, for I hated sewing; buttons were always coming adrift and the uniform I was to wear for my exam must be above reproach. Delighted to be in favour again she bounced off my bed, and as she hared down the corridor I could hear her carolling her Christmas concert song. And it was supposed to be so hush-hush until the first performance!

That day Gina and I papered her living room, and by the time we had finished clearing up it was nearly nine o'clock. I fetched a fish-and-chip supper from the corner shop and we ate it out of the paper to save washing up, after which it was a mad dash to get back to the hospital before the doors were locked at ten. As I hurried off, Gina's good wishes reminded me of my forthcoming ordeal.

It was very parky and a chill mist drifted in from the sea; hardly a night to wait for buses. As I went along at a jog trot, gas-mask case bumping rhythmically against my rump, the streets were dark and all the windows shuttered. I was nearly home and dry before the darkened bus rumbled by and was glad I had walked.

I had nearly reached the hospital gates when I passed the dark shape of an army truck pulled up at the roadside; probably some soldier and his girl croodling together. A few yards further on a darkish patch in the road caused me to pause and shine my torch. I went over to it and found an unconscious female, still alive despite severe head injuries. I tried to think what I must do, remembering that internal injuries were sometimes inflicted by the indiscriminate moving of accident cases, but all I could think was that a bus

108

was due from the opposite direction and that she lay in the path of it. I took off my cloak, spread it out beside her, and gently eased her on to it. A pochette, a small envelope-type handbag commonly used at that time, lay on the road and I picked it up, since it might have some form of identification. As I dragged her to the kerb, two dark shapes stumbled from the vicinity of the army truck: soldiers, young and frightened in the torchlight. With their dimmed truck lights they had seen nothing, only felt the impact, and now as he realized what had happened, the driver began to vomit. The other soldier helped me to lift her onto the grass verge and as we did so the darkened bus to town trundled past without stopping.

When I pointed out the hospital gates and asked them to tell the hall porter and bring a stretcher, the soldiers hurried off, heartened to have something constructive to do. As I sat with the injured girl's head in my lap, the grey mist wreathing us and white frost rimming the grasses, blood seeped stickily through my thin skirt. It was obvious she was dying. Somewhere, people as yet unknown would mourn tonight.

I wondered if there was any form of identification; her clothes were sodden with mud and blood and her face was just a pulp, but there was the pochette. It revealed only a screwed up handkerchief with a sixpence knotted in the corner, a bus ticket and a folded newspaper cutting. I smoothed it out and in the waning torchlight eerily saw a photograph of myself. I knew it well; it had featured in a daily paper, snapped to my great discomfiture when I attended survivors from a ship-wreck. I had felt a right Charlie and had suffered much ragging in consequence. What a coincidence! Maybe she had known the man I was attending to. Carefully I refolded the cutting and put it back. Soon wavering storm lanterns and the tramp of feet heralded the arrival of the stretcher. I wrapped the girl more closely in my cloak to conceal from the boy soldiers the dreadful injuries, but when we reached the entrance hall the dim blackout lights revealed little except that she was in extremis.

The night staff, already alerted, took over. 'You'd better go and get cleaned up,' said night sister, viewing me with some distaste. 'And take those noisy girls to task.'

Wild sounds were floating down from the nurses' quarters. It sounded like an Irish wake. In the common-room I found a crowd of juniors surrounding one of their contemporaries who appeared to be having hysterics. There was a sudden respectful silence when I walked in until the hysterical one, catching sight of me, gory and dishevelled in the sudden light, set off again with her banshee wailing. Heartily I slapped her down until she sobered up sufficiently to sob out her story.

'It was our evening off and we went to the pictures. When we came back on the bus, Babe ran straight across the road . . .'

The jigsaw of events was falling into a horrific pattern. That bloodstained bundle, the poor battered face, the photograph of myself! What a blind idiot I had been! Slowly, like a zombie, I turned and walked back down the stairs.

At last, when all was said and done and I escaped to my room, there laid out on the bed was Babe's last act of homage: my clean uniform, painstakingly patched and with every button in place. I found out later she had cut them off her own uniform to replace the missing ones. When I wore it the next morning the harsh starched calico lining gave the rough satisfaction of a hair skirt.

Silently we set off for Canterbury, and as we waited at the bus-stop we tried to avert our eyes from the bloodstain on the road. It had run down into the gutter to trickle wastefully into the nearest drain and later, despite our efforts with buckets of water and bleaches, it persisted, a mute reminder until the snows came and covered it.

At Canterbury we found the great white hospital, once the pride and joy of our rivals, was camouflaged a dirty grey and all its beauty gone. We never could recall what questions were asked of us or what duties we had to perform, but afterwards we turned into the cathedral and sat in silent contemplation. Christmas came and went; no one would ever sing Babe's song. All staff festivities were cancelled and instead of gifts to each other we contributed to a memorial picture for the little chapel. The war had caught up with us, and Babe was only the first to go.

*   *   *

At the end of January our exam results came through proclaiming Pansy, Moke and myself State Registered Nurses. Torti, the pick of the bunch, had failed. She accepted it philosophically, but we were stunned by the injustice of it all. The patients cheered when we self-consciously went on duty in our black petersham belts and with strings and a bow added to our Sister Dora caps. Actually they were not attached to the caps as everyone imagined, but were just a length of starched tape with a ready-made bow stitched on halfway along. The bow was placed under the chin and the two ends of tape tied on top of the head, after which the starched white cap was placed on top (and surreptitiously secured with a hatpin). The prim unyielding bow scratched constantly under the chin, as did the harsh tape behind the ears, but the little knot on top of the head was worst of all, for there was constant friction resulting eventually in a little bald patch where the hair was worn away.

I was by now on night duty again, but this time as 'runner', which meant that I was a general factotum helping out wherever needed, visiting each ward in turn to check drugs, assisting in theatre, handmaiden to night sister and Cass. The pace was fierce, but it was great. Cass had heard of the fiasco of my 21st and when my birthday came round again, he made it an excuse for celebration. He provided the drinks and eats, and night sister gave her blessing. She commanded more respect amongst the staff then anyone, and when she stipulated soft drinks only for the night staff and 'no nonsense' for the day staff she knew her word was law. Moreover she could keep an eye on Cass's intake, which was a welcome change! The patients were given the option of sherry or Black Jack when the medicine trolley went round, and at supper next morning night sister produced a bottle of vintage wine for good conduct. I decided it was worth a nose bleed.

One night when we went down to breakfast we heard that during the day the Royal Navy had arrived unheralded and carried off Stoker and Gun-layer. We felt quite disconsolate; things wouldn't be the same without them. After a few days, however, they reappeared, for their base was only at nearby Chatham and they were being given survivor's leave. After so long the hospital felt like home, and it was only natural to come back. Everyone was delighted to see them and even matron unbent a little, though she now had to forfeit her £2 a day.

When they arrived we had just gone up to our quarters but were called down to see them.

Gun-layer manoeuvred me into a corner. 'Let's get married,' he said urgently.

'But who'd have us?' I asked.

They stayed around for some time, then Stoker went home to London where he was promptly knocked down by a taxi and wrote to say he was back in hospital with fifteen stitches in his leg. It was one of matron's most rigorous rules that we should not go out with ex-patients, but one morning before going to bed I went with Gun-layer to 'The Smuggler', famous for home-made scones topped with thick cream and home-made jam. Their stocks hadn't yet run out, but it was unfortunate that the ass. mat. should have chosen the same time to go. When I got back she was waiting to usher me into the matron's office. I didn't repeat the error!

The long harsh winter still raged without abatement and bleak winds scoured the coast. No wonder the local herrings were distinguished by their blue gills! February brought the snow, silently, stealthily by night, concealing the camouflaged buildings, the stacked sandbags, the stain on the road, and bringing traffic to a standstill. Few people got through to the hospital, except one of the honorary

112

surgeons in a red pom-pom hat, proud of his prowess on skis, and Gun-layer.

Gun-layer had been assigned to another ship, the *Jarvis Bay*. It was a good berth, he said, and before long he hoped to be a gunner's mate.

Gradually the roads cleared, but the snow lingered on into March. Food rationing had begun and with it our diet improved. We had never had butter before!

There was an uneasy quiet in the war situation; beds became vacant and hospital waiting lists began to get attention again. Like all hospitals we had malingerers, and one such was Burper Belcher, one of our regulars. He might cry wolf once too often and damn us forever with a rejected perforated appendix, but when he arrived at two o'clock one morning simulating agony, Cass, unacquainted with him, was inveigled into admitting him for observation. Mr Belcher liked nothing better than to be observed. He was most proficient in making his thermometer register incorrectly if attended by the unwary, in regulating his respirations, and in swallowing air so that he became a distended wind-bag punctuating the night with eructations.

After submitting happily to a week of intensive investigation which revealed nothing abnormal, the Burper, blissfully somnolent after an injection of distilled water, fell out of bed and Torti, unable to budge him and fearful he might at last have done himself a mischief, summoned help. Cass and I arrived simultaneously to find him prone on the floor and with stertorous breathing. Cass made a cursory examination before taking a jug of iced water from an adjoining locker and pouring it over him. Mr Belcher sat up spluttering and very aggrieved. 'Sorry, old chap,' said Cass cheerfully, 'seems there's nothing can be done for your condition.' He took down the chart and scrawled across the still vacant space for diagnosis, 'Oscillans Plumbi,' and later on I saw the Burper surreptitiously copying it onto a scrap of paper. Tomorrow he would go home a happy man, boasting an affliction for which science knew no cure. I did hope that no Latin linguist would ever enlighten him!

Cass, always something of a tippler, had now begun to make merry with associates in the town. Oftentimes he would just make it to the driveway, where he would sit rendering bawdy rugger songs in his fruity Irish brogue until night sister and I hurried down to winkle him out of the tin lizzie and lug himself upstairs to his quarters, there to lock him in and pray that we wouldn't have need of him. Not unnaturally, after such bouts he became sullen and belligerent. At one time he suspected a porter of making free with his liquor and to catch the culprit doctored a bottle with croton oil (a most drastic purgative which promotes excruciating peristalsis). Then coming home inebriated, he drank it himself! Nemesis indeed! For several nights he traipsed around two-double with pain, filching alleviates from the medicine cupboards and swearing abstinence.

Of course it didn't last. Then came the crunch. Matron was away for a few days when Cass chose to entertain his friends. Sounds of revelry pervaded the first floor and indignant thumpings on his door by the ass. mat. evoked no response until 2 a.m. when it flew open and a conglomeration of young medicos in their underpants erupted on to the corridor. Hairy appendages with door-knocker knees and torsos like doormats; small wonder male nudes never caught on!

Most were known to us but were quite unrecognizable since they all wore gas-masks. Like Circe's swine they swarmed downstairs and from the sounds below it was obvious they were doing a round of the wards. Cries of 'Brandy! Brandy! Whoopee!' indicated the medicine cupboards were being raided. In no time at all they were back upstairs and trooping along to the male surgical ward, followed by the ass. mat. wringing her hands and night sister wrathful and incredulous at having her authority flouted.

I was working on the female surgical ward, the nurse there being unwell, and there were a number of very ill patients. Drawn out in the corridor by the carousal, I was joined by Nurse Donna, one of the evacuee nurses who was

114

in charge of the children's ward next door. We stared at each other aghast; obviously we were next on the list. Bella (she just had to be Bella) breathed heavily down her nose. 'Navair, in mine country could such a thing come to pass,' she snorted, but this was no time for censure. There were no locks on the double doors leading to the wards, only large 'grab' handles on the inside of them, so the thing was to tie the handles securely together. Bandages were not strong enough, so we took off our long black woollen stockings. Bella went inside her ward and wove her stockings through and around the handles, finishing with a tight knot. I pushed hard but the doors stood firm. Hurriedly I went into my ward and did the same just as the mob arrived. Furious and frustrated, they clamoured and pushed, while from my side I pushed back. Our stockings were tough and durable. The doors parted slightly and as a hand snaked through I bit hard on it and it was withdrawn with a yowl of pain and indignation. Eventually the rabble went away. They were beginning to sober up and there was quiet except for a whimpering from some of the patients.

Matron was recalled the next morning. There was a board meeting and poor, foolish, talented Cass walked the wards no more.

* * *

The inclement weather persisted and the cold was still intense; most opportune, matron decided, for me to take my long overdue holidays. I decided to visit an ex-colleague in Cambridge and the short time left to me was fraught with preparation. By the time my holiday began, I was exhausted. Gun-layer, still marking time before sailing, promised to see me at the station. I would still have to travel via London, he said.

Of course I missed my train, but Gun-layer was still waiting. He had, he explained, got leave. It was marriage leave. (In fact if he returned unwed, there would be the devil to pay!) He was armed with a special licence. That must have cost him a pretty packet. I could never abide waste.

The station was crowded. I was not sure if there were more people travelling or just less trains, but I was indescribably weary and had the feeling that the world was going round anti-clockwise. Gun-layer, ever practical, suggested that he should join the long queue at the ticket office while I made inquiries as to the time of departure and platform for the London train. Everyone seemed to be trying to find out the same thing, and there appeared to be no means of finding out. A rather aloof porter stood well away from the milling throng doing absolutely nothing, but when I approached him with my query, he looked down his nose at me and said: 'I really don't know, madam.'

'But you should know,' I cried. 'It's your job to know.' I became more heated when he raised a cynical eyebrow and gave him a few more home truths until I caught sign of Gun-layer from a distance signalling agitatedly.

Petulantly I walked over to him. 'Hey, what are you doing talking to our chief petty officer?' he said.

We were married at Caxton Hall. Gun-layer bought the ring en route and also a hat, which he considered was an essential for me. It was a Marina-green pill-box affair. I cannot remember which dress I wore, but I think it was one I had bought off Moke for two bob after she had scorched a large hole in the back. I had always admired the front, and the back didn't show with a coat on. We had quite forgotten the need for witnesses, but a Canadian soldier and his girl, who had just braved the Atlantic to marry him, offered their services. Their names were Hilda and John. We had a meal together afterwards and never saw them again.

London was brave and cheerful under the blackout. Gun-layer was quite affluent with his accumulation of back pay (and I had all of ten bob!). We saw the latest shows: *Gulliver's Travels*, *The Wizard of Oz* and the Crazy Gang singing 'Run Rabbit Run', with the very rabbit (so they assured us), which had been the first air-raid casualty of the war.

I had wired my friend at Cambridge and perfidiously sent her my mail for re-posting. Meanwhile we were staying at a little hotel in Westminster, quite cut off from the world we knew. The proprietors were kindly indulgent, but I was thrown into turmoil when they offered to get the name changed on my ration book. Matron would throw a fit.

I returned to day-duty, staffing on the medical wing, and wondered what would happen if they found out? Married nurses were quite taboo. Gun-layer was again in limbo, for during our absence the *Jarvis Bay* had sailed without him, unexpectedly and under secret orders. He mourned inordinately, but she and all his shipmates had gone to a glorious end and complete annihilation. He still haunted the vicinity during his free time but soon he was assigned to another ship and was gone. It was as though he had never been, except for a wedding ring on a bit of string around my neck.

This was to set the pattern of our lives, for during the next six years we were destined to spend less than six months together. Leaves were so often given abroad, in Australia and in Capetown (home of the Captain!). Letters were infrequent and censored. One night, after duty, I confided in Gentle Jane. We had always been close and I knew she would never tell. One day Stoker came to see us again. Gun-layer, he warned us, was now a married man, the sly old salt! Oh well, you know what sailors are! Everyone looked pityingly at me. I was glad I had told Jane.

I had kept in touch with my old hospital via my friend Wallybags, who was now staffing there. Wally could never be persuaded to write letters and I always enclosed the reply to my epistle, giving alternatives to my queries so that she had only to delete what was irrelevant and post it. Now I had a letter from my former matron offering me the position of relief sister there. When I showed it to matron, she advised me to take it, at least temporarily, for it was obvious that many of us would have to go elsewhere during the uncertain conditions, and so I accepted it.

The old clique was breaking up and we went our various ways. Pansy Plant was off to London where she had an excellent post and a date with a doodle-bug; Torti Collis had to find another training school from which to resit her State Final, and Moke, bewitched by the posters, succumbed to nursing the senior service and was soon drafted abroad to die miserably of an obscure fever. Jane, an only child, had to take a job which would also enable her to care for her semi-invalid widowed mother.

I found my old stamping ground surprisingly the same. It was I who had changed. The old folk at home were delighted to have me near again; their welcome embraced me, but I was consumed with guilt, for I still could not bring myself to confess my espousement and the wedding ring hung like a millstone round my neck.

When I had relieved each of the ward sisters in turn, I took on night sister's duties, for Calamity had retired and had not been replaced. The area was as yet unbreached by bombs but pestered with alerts when enemy planes passed over en route for richer targets. The urgency of the alerts was indicated by a code of colours given via the phone; when it reached red all the staff were roused and the patients, on their heavy iron frames or in cumbersome plaster cases, were placed under their beds from where they all immediately demanded bedpans! Meanwhile down in the village the vicar ran about like one demented, ringing a hand-bell and calling his flock to shelter.

It was decided to equip each of us with a pass which would enable us to return unhindered if we were caught out during raids. These were like glorified passports, bearing a photograph together with our credentials, and we had to present ourselves with them in matron's office in order that she might add her signature to verify their authenticity.

As she was about to sign mine, I felt impelled to stay her. 'It's incorrect,' I said lamely, and she waited unperturbed, pen still poised, for an explanation. When I had given it she was, as ever, practical and uncondemning. She offered to get my name altered on everything documental, but stipulated that in return I must tell my parents without further delay. I had no option now, and they accepted the confession as being typical of my wilfulness and hid their hurt, so that I was more conscience-stricken than ever. At matron's suggestion I began to bank my off-duty against such time as my husband should get leave, and as the months passed it totted up encouragingly.

We all listened to the traitorous voice of Lord Haw-Haw, and waxed hilarious at his menacing implications, but sometimes he was more informative than the nine o'clock news. One night he alluded threateningly to Gun-layer's ship: 'Germany calling! Germany calling! We are after you *Sussex*, we know of your whereabouts.' It was more than I did!

'Jaysus!' ejaculated Wallybags, crossing herself piously. 'Bad cess to the blackguards and bring the boyo home!'

Her prayer was answered, for a few days later I had a phone call from Gun-layer himself and he was home! His ship had docked at Liverpool for supplies and the crew had high hopes of leave, for it was obvious they were due for a long spell at sea, but when none was forthcoming and they were about to sail again, someone (it was never discovered who) threw a spanner in the turbines rendering the great ship helpless and at the mercy of the raiders who had tracked her down. The crew were dispersed until she could be repaired and their unknown benefactor was the toast of them all. Gun-layer, unsure of where I might be, had sent a telegram which father had apprehensively opened and then met him at the station. The parents, said my husband, were being very hospitable. Mother said she had known they would have a visitor for she had dropped a knife on the floor and also there had been a 'stranger on the bars' of the fireplace.

I claimed my accumulated leave and was given permission to go home, but as I sat in the train a terrible thought struck me. My husband would be waiting for me at the station, but what if I did not recognize him? It had been an awful long time. I tried to visualize him and could not. A currently popular song, 'The Sailor With The Navy Blue Eyes', pursued me. What colour were his? I hauled my baggage off the rack and under cover of the lid rummaged for his photograph. Anxiously I scrutinized it and was immediately reassured. Of course! He would still have the large indented scar on his forehead.

Would he recognize me? Perhaps I should have told him I would wear a red carnation or something. But when I stepped down onto the old familiar platform there was no confusion. He was in uniform.

They were halcyon days and it was summertime. We climbed Clent Hills, lay on the sunbaked plateau of Kinver Edge and picnicked on Penn Common, but I was anguished by the mutilated stumps of Baggeridge Woods. People ran to touch Gun-layer's broad sailor collar for luck, and we remembered with gratitude our unknown benefactor, the spanner-thrower. Gun-layer had brought me twenty-four pairs of sheer silk stockings from America and I purred at such luxury; they flattered the new short skirts too, for we had been cautioned to economize on materials and had patriotically raised our hems to help the war effort.

We made a brief pilgrimage to London, sunbathing by the Serpentine in Green Park and in Kensington Gardens; only the almost imperceptible hum of distant traffic betrayed the Great Metropolis around us. Of course we stayed at the little hideout in Westminster, thereby establishing our respectability, which seemed important to Gun-layer. The small hotel enfolded us in its warm embrace for the last time. We would come again, we said. But when we finally did so, we found only a hole in the ground.

Travelling back, the train was crowded with child evacuees, all hung about with little treasures and labelled like small parcels for alien destinations. After the first few tearful miles their natural resilience took over and they chatted intrepidly of the adventures ahead. Those in our compartment carried buckets and spades as part of their equipment for they were, they said excitedly, being sent to the seaside. Laconically their labels proclaimed 'DUDLEY PORT'.

Gun-layer, whose parents had divorced when he was a child, was a Yorkshireman. Next time, he said, we would

explore the Dales, the Butter-tubs, the old Roman encamp-
ments and the Cock-Beck, which had run red with blood
during the Wars of the Roses, and we would walk together
on Ilkley moor 'bar t'at'.

Finally came the last evening, the last possible train.
Father was fire-watching and mother had diplomatically
gone to visit one of her cronies. One thing my husband
never had was mother-in-law problems. Reluctantly we set
off for the station.

'Wish me luck as you wave me goodbye,' pleaded a
nearby radio.

'Is your journey really necessary?' demanded the railway
posters.

We waited on the same platform from which for years I
had embarked unwillingly to school in Wolverhampton,
thinking myself a well-seasoned traveller. Wolverhampton!
Gun-layer had sailed the world over, had taken part in
running the Spanish blockade and spent four years in
Palestine. The radio had changed to plaintive strains of
'Harbour Lights'. The train came and he was gone. Had he
ever been?

Tomorrow I must go back to hospital, but now I went to
collect Mother from her friend's house. It was a night of
dangerous moonlight and we were halfway home when the
sirens began to wail; their high-pitched lamentations
always exhilarated me and I felt guilty because of it. There
was no available shelter ahead, but Mother would never
retrace her steps. It was bad luck to turn back!

First came the incendiary bombs, illuminating the landscape and drawing raiders in their wake like moths to the
flames. The ominous drone of aircraft was followed by the
crunch of heavier bombs, and from the searchlight batteries
fingers of light probed the sky, trapping within their beams
a tiny silver plane.

The ack-ack guns began a clangorous chatter and
shrapnel spattered metallically around us.

Mother paused just long enough to put up her umbrella.

*   *   *

121

In no time at all I knew that I was pregnant. I shared out the stockings and resolved to hide my condition as long as possible. It was not easy; I was the only married member of the community and under constant surveillance by the others. Wallybags speculated openly and asked impertinent questions, for her sister had double-jointed twins and she considered herself an authority on the subject.

'Bejapers!' she asserted, 'Sure, it's plain on your dial, no need for a conspicuous belliosis.' In vain I protested that I was in fact losing weight.

'The slope before the bank!' declared Wally, and began knitting little pants because it was sure to be 'a broth of a boy'.

By now the red alerts were constant. During the last three weeks I was there we kipped uneasily in odd corners and never went to bed at all.

Sadly, for the last time, I said goodbye to the hospital. Halfway home the train halted and we were told that no more trains would get through that night. There was no seating accommodation and with the stopping of the train the feeble lights were doughted and the heating discontinued. It was a long, cold night, and bonded together by a common misery we stamped about, blowing on our numbed fingers and awed by the terrible magnificence of the skies ahead. It was Coventry ablaze.

When he heard of my redundancy, my father-in-law wrote from a remote village in Yorkshire suggesting that I might like to housekeep for himself and my young brother-in-law. He did not know what he was letting himself in for; I had no domesticity. But still, if I did not know how to cook, at least I knew how to treat them for indigestion! So I went alone to the Dales and the Cock-Beck and Ilkley moor 'bar t'at'.

I was intrigued and delighted to find that they drank tea from colourful pint pots decorated with mottos; mine bore the legend:

Hear all, see all, say nowt,

Above left and right: Honeymooners in London, March 1940

ove left: Gunlayer with Judith, 1947 *Above right:* Self with Elizabeth and Judith, 1947

Gunlayer and Judith, 1962

Eat all, sup all, pay nowt,
An' when tha does owt fer nowt,
Allus do it fer thissen.

But the caption on the back was more brief and to the point. 'Take hod and sup,' it instructed, and so I did.

In the village, where everyone knew everyone else, I was vetted, dissected and reassembled with the precision of experts, and the housewives hastened to disclose the dedicated doctrine of making Yorkshire pudding. It precluded every midday meal on a plate of its own and consecrated with rich gravy.

They all spoke like telegrams, missing out the little words, and the 'Co-op' was their religion. I once saw a van bearing the slogan: 'Bury by the Co-op and collect the Divi!'

Most of the men worked in the pits, except my brother-in-law who was apprenticed out in Leeds. Pop-in-law, who was delighted by the prospect of becoming a grandparent, was in charge of the pit ponies; lovingly he doctored and groomed them and saved tit-bits to take with his 'snap'. It was a sad day if he had to use the 'humane killer' and his snap came back unopened. During the holiday period when the ponies were brought above ground for a brief spell, he would take us to see them cavorting in the fields, kicking up their legs, delirious with joy to feel the green grass and the sunlight.

I soon chummed up with the local district nurse who did just about everything. Trained nurses were hard to come by and she was delighted to have help with her clinics and, when confinements were imminent, to be able to pass on to me the colostomies, carcinomas and laying-outs – and also her own small daughter when she was called out at night.

Meanwhile iron gates and railings were commandeered to be smelted down for raw materials. Wrapping paper was scarce and we embroidered white huckaback in which to collect our rations and vied with each other in the queues as to whose was the whitest. I yearned for fresh fruit, but it was unobtainable; ships had more important cargoes than

123

oranges for fanciful females. Tomatoes, when available, were seven shillings a pound. We were told to extract the juice from raw swedes, gather rose hips in season, and it was hinted that if we consumed raw carrots we would see better in the blackout!

My daughter was born on 15 May 1941, seven years to the day on which I had set out on my career. It was the first time I had been in hospital on the wrong side of the blanket. I had not heard from Gun-layer for several months and it transpired later that he was part of a skeleton crew that had been transferred to a German prize ship and then lost trace of. (Pop-in-law sent him a wire announcing his daughter's arrival, but she was nine months old when he finally received it!)

War news was despondent and there was talk of invasion. Hitler had a secret weapon. A deadly dysentery was rampant amongst the new-born. What a heritage! I looked down at my little bundle. It was a bleak world I had brought her into: a missing father, an irresponsible mother, no hope of a home for years to come.

Then I cheered up again. After all, I thought, it's not everyone who can trace their beginnings to a spanner in the turbines!

My father-in-law was proud to become a grandparent and spent hours pram-pushing in the countryside. He saw in Elizabeth a likeness to his own mother about whom he was very nostalgic, for although he was her only child she had cast him out after his marriage at eighteen and he never saw her again.

When hostilities ended letters from abroad were un-censored, and we knew now where our menfolk were. Gun-layer was as far away as could be, with no chance of leave at home. He and his shipmates spent their leave on convenient tropical islands; they were, he said, as brown as the natives, 'except amidships'.

Inexorably the years passed. The war was over and with it our youth.

CHAPTER SEVEN

— My Little Black Bag —

G UN-LAYER HAD been a sailor man and boy, though not of course in that order. Now he was on his way home from the Far East; his current ship the *Manxman*, whose record was one of the most remarkable of the war, was known as the racehorse of the Royal Navy and in no time I was waiting apprehensively for his train. It seemed as though our marriage had been conducted on the platforms of railway stations, but despite this and without undue promulgation we had produced a daughter.

We had both changed, he from a youthful twelve stone to a mature fifteen, me from a rounded ten to a scrawny eight and a half. His new uniform and officer-type peaked cap became him; he was now a gunner's mate, superior in rank to the Gun-layer I had married, but I clung to the familiar title as a drowner to a straw.

While mourning my depleted curves I had other things to offer and one was the key to our very first front door, for under the new points system we had qualified for a Tarren prefabricated bungalow and with my accumulated earnings and extra furniture vouchers (swapped for precious clothing coupons), I had just managed to equip it cash down.

Another of Gun-layer's dreams had materialized into a substantial five-year-old daughter, but whatever illusions he'd cherished about Elizabeth it was obvious he was stunned by her solidity, and the tiny silk Japanese

125

garment he had brought for her would not have accommodated a child of two. She was waiting for us at home, and when they met father and daughter eyed each other suspiciously. I had told her about him and given her photographs but she did not understand.

'There's two uncles and two grandads,' she argued. 'Why is there only one Daddy?'

Now he stood before her in the flesh, solid, proffering gifts and with a false jocularity. She took the presents silently and retired with them behind the settee. Obviously relieved by her withdrawal he turned to me, spreading his arms wide, but from the hidey-hole her eyes watched us covertly and I evaded him.

The wasted years had dealt more kindly with him. His attractions were still there, the dark eyes, the cleft chin, the deep scar now bleached by the tropical sun, but I felt suddenly old and very inadequate. Disgruntled he flung himself into a chair.

While preparing a meal I pondered on the problem. It was obvious we would have to start again from scratch but would we, just meeting for the first time, have chosen each other now? Peering critically at my reflection I decided I wouldn't have chosen me.

'They don't make mirrors like they used to,' I complained ruefully, and GL chortled as though recognizing some essential characteristic.

'You'll do!' he laughed and we embraced for the first time.

*   *   *

A double bed is in itself an institution and the next morning we overslept, surely a good omen? I woke to find Elizabeth standing at the bedside staring at GL's dark head upon the pillow.

'You told me he slept in a hammock!' she cried accusingly.

Later when she was ready for school and he waited to

126

escort her, she walked primly beside him without trotting out her usual string of excuses.

'But I haven't got to *keep* going have I?'

'I'm sure it's Saturday.'

'I feel pale.'

'My elastic's broke.'

I had several days off from my job in deference to GL so we went to the shops in search of the luxuries which were beginning to filter through, for the war had been over more than a year now. If you saw a queue you joined it, and we did so and were lucky. After shuffling forward for about an hour (and buying provisions we didn't really want, to qualify), we were each allowed one banana. Corn in Egypt! We bore them home triumphantly for Elizabeth.

When we collected her from school her teacher told us that in class during the daily family-news-items she had offered her contribution solemnly.

'I've got a Daddy. He's come home and he's got fevvers on his chest.'

When she had the first of her bananas Elizabeth was delighted. What a change from the customary wartime 'banana sandwiches' made from mashed parsnips flavoured with banana essence. We had to show her how to peel off the 'sleeve', for many children when first confronted with them ate the lot! They have remained her favourite fruit and she never tires of them.

*   *   *

Gun-layer had joined the Royal Navy straight from school at the age of sixteen but years of service were not then taken into account until the 21st birthday, and now he had twelve months to serve in Chatham barracks as a gunnery instructor. To leave his ship must have been a wrench. I felt I was a poor substitute for a mistress who boasted 72,000 h.p. Originally commissioned in June 1941, the 4,000-ton minelayer *Manxman* was one of four ships specially designed with a low silhouette to get close into enemy shores. When in December 1942 she was torpedoed and sustained a cavity on her engine side through which a car could have been driven, she had limped the hundred miles to shore and lived to avenge the loss of her three sister ships. In eighteen months she laid 3,000 mines, though she was capable of laying 156 in nine minutes during an emergency. The secret of a successful sortie was to accomplish the mission without being detected by the enemy and so camouflage was of paramount importance. Once after the collapse of France, disguised as a French merchantman with a false bow, she had laid mines off the Italian coast while her crew, dressed as Frenchies, even to the red bobbles on their caps, and with washing fluttering traditionally from the decks, cheekily laughed off challenges made by French, Italian and German ships before making their getaway. Another time, concealed with webbing, she was transformed into a coral island.

However her activities were not always confined to the laying of lethal eggs. She was also instrumental in bringing back survivors from the *Ark Royal*, and when Malta was at starvation point she was the first ship to reach her in three months. As she sailed in with a cargo of dried milk and concentrated food, women fell on their knees and held up their children to see their triumphant entry into Grand Harbour. Afterwards the crew emptied their own canteen to give a party for the thousand orphan children of the island.

GL was never one to speak of his experiences, but once war was over the press had gone to town relating exploits of interest and the *Manxman*'s homecoming had made it a point of focal concern. He took umbrage to such exposure.

The motto beneath the *Manxman*'s crest of the three-legged man, 'Whichever way you throw it, it stands up', was appropriate for him too, for he got used to being home quicker than we got used to having him. For over five years we had muddled on together in a happy-go-lucky way, now everything had to be shipshape and Bristol fashion, there was a place for everything and everything must be in its place. Consequently we could never find anything because it had all been tidied away; in the small confines of a ship this was essential but this was our home and we rebelled. Poor GL! Instead of a crew of submissive subordinates he now had two wilful womenfolk refusing to toe the line. I've heard it said by naval men that gunner's mates are a race apart and ours was no exception.

I was astounded to see the amount of liquor he could consume with no apparent ill effect, but he had been weaned on the Navy's traditional daily tot of very potent rum and as he said, 'You're not drunk so long as you can lie on the floor without holding on.'

When I returned to my job at a day nursery he came into his own, polished the brasses and lavatory seat and consigned our whole meat ration for a week to one dish. Nothing daunted, the next day he bought steaks of whale meat (unrationed), which he braised with onions and declared delicious. He had a way with shopkeepers and one day came home with a whole ox tail. Wallybags who came to visit us still talks of the fantastic soup he made for her.

When at last Gun-layer's leave was over and he went back to barracks we settled into our old routine. The weeks passed as before and it was as though he had never been, but he had, there was proof: this time next year we would be four instead of three.

The maternity dress had lain fallow for over five years. It was green with lace ruffles at the wrist and throat. Hilda had made it and worn it for Margaret, her one ewe lamb, and then bequeathed it to me for Elizabeth. Now it would come into its own again. I was sad to leave the nursery where I had been so happy for over three years but the reason for my going made it all worth while. At last I would have time for Elizabeth; this baby would free me for myself. I saw a vista of fruitful years ahead and I was filled with a creative urge. Gleefully I gave in my notice.

'Why the haste?' asked the MOH with amused tolerance. Surely I could wait until they had a replacement? He was a bachelor. What did he know of fanciful females? The itch to knit, the need to dream, the morning sickness? Submissively I acquiesced; I've always been a doormat. I was deputy matron at the day nursery and it was a very happy establishment. We took seventy children from nought to five for the charge of 1s a day (5p today), and we were open six days a week from 7.30 a.m. to 7.30 p.m. except Saturdays, when we closed at midday. The aim had been to release mothers for war work, with priority being given to one-parent families, but though the war was over we still had a long waiting list of applicants. Despite food rationing three main meals a day with sundry snacks were part of the service and the kitchen staff excelled with appetizing dishes.

The baby nursery was in the charge of my friend Joyce who was a trained nursery nurse, and when the mothers brought their little bundles, snug and sleepy straight from their cots, they knew that they would be already prepared for bed when they collected them at night and that between whiles they would be loved and cosseted as if they were her own.

I had been able to take Elizabeth with me in the beginning and now that she was at school she was able to come to us out of school hours, but of course there had to be no discrimination and she always called me Sister as did the other children, and she continued to do so at home. This was one of the things that GL found very disconcerting. Constantly he corrected her but she was very stubborn; having been reluctantly landed with a 'Father' she was not anxious to be lumbered with a 'Mother' as well.

One Saturday afternoon we went to the Brummagem sales and rummaged amongst the baby wear. It was all 'slightly soiled' or 'imperfect' and our baby warranted the best. As always when I go to sales I came away with something that had not been reduced: a cot blanket of the softest fleece and heavenly blue. Why blue when I knew it would be a girl? It was the only one, displayed desirably upon a stand and all of ten bob, and I couldn't resist it.

Friday was always hectic, a day on which the mothers tended to collect their offspring late for it was wages day and they liked to get their shopping done first. This Friday was no exception and I was thankful when the last child had been claimed. It had been a long day for Elizabeth too and I was looking forward to a hot bath and an early night. Once home I shed my uniform and went to run the bath.

'Daddy's home,' said Elizabeth gloomily, coming out of the loo.

'Whatever makes you think that?' I asked amazed.

'Seat's up.' she announced laconically, and sure enough when I peeked through the window there was GL laboriously raking over the patch of rubble that was our garden. He looked caggy and rather pathetic with a spade and his feet were in the wrong place. 'Leave that,' I cried, 'I've got something exciting to tell you.'

* * *

I progressed into blue smocks with white collars while waiting for my replacement but I was surrounded by friends, both mothers and staff, who were concerned for my welfare. It was made obvious to me that I could have leave and return with the baby but I felt I knew now where I was going and I was determined to do my own thing.

Although the war was over there were disturbing elements abroad. Most of us had been shocked and horrified by the dropping of atom bombs on Japan and had a deep sense of guilt although we'd had no say in the decision. Now we were told that the winds bearing the radioactivity of that crime had reached us. Strontium-90 was at its highest in Wales, and our guilt was coloured with a foreboding that was later to be fulfilled in my own family.

I was nearly seven months pregnant when I finally got my release. Gun-layer had planned to have part of his leave when the baby was due but as soon as I went into labour he rushed me into hospital and then made a clean getaway. Fathers, he said, were essential at the laying of the keel but were quite superfluous at the launching. Gun-layer had broad shoulders but they were not intended to cry on.

Our second daughter was born on 10 May and she was so like him he forgave her for not being a boy. While we were in hospital Elizabeth had her sixth birthday, and I had left a life-size baby doll complete with layette. It was her first real doll for they had been unobtainable until then, except rag ones, usually home-made. She was staying with Mother and Dad who doted on her and whom she loved dearly.

*　　*　　*

After the long severe winter spring had come with a flourish. As we took home 'a sister for Elizabeth' the driver chose a quiet unfrequented route from Gornal where she had been born. It was a day of promise and primroses and spring sunshine.

GL's sister Lilian was to be one of the godmothers at the christening. Her second name was Victoria and I thought it would be a compliment to her to choose it; however it was revealed that she disliked it intensely and favoured Judith, as did GL, so Judith it was.

GL returned reluctantly to barracks when his leave was over, loath to leave her lest she should mature behind his back as Elizabeth had done and take him unawares. There wasn't much fear of that for his contract with the navy terminated in July. If he agreed to sign on again he would get promotion and a substantial pension in ten years, but he had made up his mind and nothing would change that. He planned to train as a teacher specializing in maths and geography at which he excelled.

The next few weeks were the happiest I'd known. I felt free and rejuvenated. Judith was such a good baby and every day we escorted Elizabeth to and from school. She loved her baby sister and showed no sign of jealousy though she could have been forgiven for doing so. Our little bungalow was well designed with two large bedrooms, a lounge and a very modern streamlined kitchen and bathroom. A gas cooker, refrigerator and immersion heater were part of the fittings and the rent was 14s a week (70p).

In July GL came home for his last leave; at the end of it his naval career was over. Although there was an unseasonal fog on the night when he should normally have returned, we went to the station and waited for his usual train. It was very late coming and the station was deserted but doggedly we waited – just for the joy of watching it go out without him.

Poor Elizabeth became very uneasy as time passed.

'He's a long time going back, isn't he?' she asked anxiously and when I tried to explain she cried in horror:

'He isn't going to *live* with us, is he?'

She was a war casualty if ever there was one.

*   *   *

GL's disappointment matched my Father's when his application for teacher training was turned down; they wanted no one over thirty. He tried several jobs before joining the ambulance service and that was his métier – he was back in uniform and the ambulance station was his ship.

We had been in the Tarren bungalow about eighteen months when those of us who had two or more children were offered houses on the new Glebefields estate. They were very presentable and GL was most anxious that we should have one, but the rent was much higher and his wages were not sufficient for us to qualify; only if I agreed to take a job would we come into that category. That I was very loath to do though there were jobs aplenty. State Registered Nurses were at a premium, and the pressure was on. The Chairwoman of the District Nurses Association was beating a pathway to our door; she was desperate for staff. Hitherto there had been three district nurses in Tipton for general work but two were expecting babies and the other was leaving for reasons of her own. The new Health Scheme was to start in six months when the Government would take over but for that six months the District Nursing Association, who had held the fort since the year dot, must throw in the towel if they could not find someone to bridge the gap.

I, said the chairlady, was that bridge. Surely I could oblige them for that short period of time? After six months I could leave with pleasure if I so wished, as the problem would then be out of their hands. When I still resisted she made other concessions: I need only work part-time. My husband she knew did shift work. I could work alternate shifts with him and then there would always be one of us at home to take charge of the baby. But I had been out of nursing for so many years. 'It will all come back to you.' she cried. 'Have no fears, anyone with an inkling of nursing can cope with district work.' With great foreboding I capitulated. Tipton had got itself half a district nurse and my husband his coveted house; we moved in on Christmas Eve and I was to commence my new job in the New Year.

How I dreaded the dawn of that day. The previous evening the remaining nurse arrived with my little black bag, which was really navy blue. I thought she looked like an avenging angel and not at all pregnant, and I wondered if she knew how terrified I was.

I had every reason to be, for medicine had changed greatly in the past eight years and ignorance set in motion is a deadly sin. Insulin alone had changed out of all recognition: in my day it had all been 20 units per c.c. and given twice daily. I had to do some quick mental arithmatic and at each diabetic I 'forgot' some small essential thing, my purse, my watch, my notebook, so that I had an excuse to return and make sure no one had gone into a coma.

The chairwoman had thrown me in at the deep end. She had also omitted to say when inveigling me to do 'part-time' that I would be doing exactly the same work as full time but for half pay. (Also that the autobikes hitherto used by the nurses were being withdrawn.)

The shift system wasn't going to work, and no one in their right mind could have expected it to. The obvious solution was the day nursery but as always there was a long waiting list. I couldn't expect to jump the queue because I had worked there, and I didn't ask.

Then came Credegwyn Llewellyn Morgan to charm us with her lilting Welsh voice and gentle demeanour and to be our friend for life. She had taken rooms nearby because her husband was working in the vicinity and she was looking for a job which would take her out of her lodgings for a part of the day. Caring for our children when we were both out was ideal for her and for them; she had the house to herself to do as she wished, and we added the key and the spare room which we could not yet afford to furnish and in which she could store the tackle which cluttered the two small rooms she and her husband were renting.

By degrees I became resigned to my job. I had not been provided with a uniform so I had my camel coat dyed navy blue and wore my old hospital gear with its stiff collars and deep starched cuffs.

'Hey up!' the local children would cry. ''ere cums the nuss with collars on 'er risses!' and they would vie with each other for the privilege of carrying my black bag which contained instruments, catheters, all kinds of syringes (even a Higginson's) and a whole range of gallipots. The case was a metal one with a waterproof cover and was no light weight for someone on foot.

The patients were supposed to provide their own dressings and all that was needed for their treatment but most of them were hard put to do it. Dressings, when you could get them, were cut to the required size, packed in large biscuit tins and baked in the oven as a semblance to sterility. Mother toured round the aunts commandeering old sheets and linen that could be used for this purpose. I found myself needing a second bag for these extras, and lugging two heavy bags around all day did little for my posture and even less for my gait.

Roseanna was one of my elderly diabetic patients who lived with her daughter and son-in-law and was dependent upon them for everything. Although they had a young family, and there were no family allowances, they begrudged her nothing, but she felt it keenly and I took to buying her insulin and slipping it in surreptitiously. Roseanna had worked hard all her life but her meagre savings were now gone and she did not qualify for the old age pension. While bequeathing her such an enviable name her parents had omitted to register her birth and so as far as the authorities were concerned she had never been born.

I told her sad tale to the social workers and they investigated, but officially she didn't exist and officialdom was above reproach. Indignantly I asked to see the Medical Officer of Health. He was a dour Scot but his indignation matched mine and he took up the cudgels on Roseanna's behalf. Her age was assessed and a grant, just sixpence less than the old age pension, was allocated to her. Better still, she was given back pay which she delighted in giving to her loyal little family.

*   *   *

My salary was £15 a month but the expenses incurred by my going out to work were in excess of that, so we were no better off financially and I'd always got a month left over at the end of my money. Other district nurses with whom I occasionally met up complained constantly of being kept waiting for theirs whilst their nursing associations had garden parties, jumbles sales and whist drives in order to collect it. Mine, on the other hand, were paying me only half salary (and no doubt had sold the autobikes to do it).

One-third of my patients were dying of pulmonary tuberculosis; most of the others were stroke cases or ulcerated legs but I found I was also expected to do the layings out, even though I had not attended the deceased, and miscarriages too were my responsibility.

'Am yo' a pregnant nus?' asked one anxious husband when his wife went into premature labour.

May had come again and with it Judith's first birthday, Elizabeth's seventh and Peg the avenging angel's new-born son. She had invited me to approach her with any queries that might arise and out of her greater experience I had learned enough to survive. We were now on Christian name terms and the six months was nearly over.

The day the Health Service began I arrived home to find my husband entertaining a formidable female wearing an impressive uniform with pips and flashes and epaulettes. She introduced herself as the senior nursing officer for Staffordshire. Tipton was part of that area and she had

136

obviously come to case the joint but I could afford to be easy
– I was leaving.

Not until they had replacements she cried, and I was
immediately suspicious – I'd heard that word somewhere
before, but of course I would hardly leave the patients
unattended. Tipton, she went on to say, had a population of
40,000 for which four general nurses were allocated. Two
had already been engaged. Peg I knew intended returning
when her son was established in the day nursery, was I
expected to be the fourth? I had a feeling the subject had
been under discussion before my arrival. The horror must
have shown on my face for she hastened to add that the
Health Scheme planned to improve the conditions of nurses
as well as patients. I had not had a day off or any leave at all
during my six months because there had been no one to
relieve me, but in future nurses would get one day off a
week, one weekend a month and increased salaries. She
sugared the pill with the prospect of a car. When we could
raise the deposit the authorities would loan the rest at 1 per
cent, docking it off my salary over a period of time until it
was repaid.

I caught the glint in Gun-layer's eye and was lost. He had
given up his deep love of the sea for me. I always was one to
sneeze at a gnat and swallow a camel.

I swallowed the camel.

*   *   *

It took an unconscionable time to save that deposit.
Meanwhile the superintendent's other predictions were
substantiated. The two new nurses materialized: bonded
friends who shared a car, a tied house and a fierce loyalty to
each other.

When there were the four of us we were summoned to a
meeting at the clinic to decide which area we should each
inherit. A large map of Tipton had been divided into four
equal parts and we all jockeyed for the bit with the
cemetery.

After the ballyhoo of the Health Scheme people became

very conscious of their rights. Everything was free and so a great deal of waste ensued, a waste which has escalated with the years.

The social workers basked in a rare popularity as they magnanimously doled out chits for clothes, bedding and various goods which were often returned to the shop for a refund by the recipients. Henery, however, was not one of these. He was a long-term patient of mine, a large lethargic man whose legs, weary of supporting his cumbersome frame, had 'broke out' in protest. I dressed them daily and bound them with crêpe bandages and, once a week, assisted by Mrs Henery, I gave him a bath.

Henery spent his days sitting in the ingle-nook of their little cottage and said nowt about owt. His wife, though her attitude towards me was always friendly, brooked no interference with her spouse, and when I suggested that exercise might stir his sluggish circulation she wanted him to stay put. When I proposed more protein and less carbohydrate in his diet, she asserted that Henery must never eat cheese or red meat. She added darkly that Henery needed watching. She always made a point of being present when I attended to him and when going shopping I noticed she was most careful, after securing the fireguard, to lock him in.

She was also very wary of visitors and always answered the door with her hat on. If the visitors were welcome she had just come in, but if they were unwelcome she was just going out.

The old age pension did not cater for extras and when Mrs Henery sighed that their blankets were getting threadbare I said not to worry, I was sure the social welfare people would oblige and I would get them to send one of their visitors.

A few days later on approaching the Henerys' home, I was amazed to see a little red mini parked outside and a vision of loveliness emerging from the front door, the dolliest of dolly-birds. Pale, gleaming, shoulder-length hair swung freely round her piquant little face and a miniscule mini-skirt displayed her shapely limbs to perfection. Dimpling endearingly she waved a farewell, swung her supple self into the mini and was gone.

I stood open-mouthed for some moments before seeing Mrs Henery, arms akimbo, astride her front doorstep.

'Got yo' ter thank for that!' she called belligerently.

This was not like Mrs Henery, so I hastened to find the cause.

'That young bessom – ' she nodded in the direction into which the vision had disappeared like a mirage. 'Welfare werker!' She spat out the word with venom.

'What – her? 'I cried ungrammatically. To me welfare worker conjured up the image of a homely little man with baggy pants and a black note-book. Things had certainly changed.

'I'm sure she's qualified,' I said lamely.

'Qualified fer what?' snarled Mrs Henery, standing aside for me to enter. I noticed then that there was something strange about Henery. He was lumbering around restlessly and when he saw me he took my hand and led me to a chair. I sat down for it was obvious that he had something momentous to impart. His eyes were glazed and he was sweating slightly when he spoke, slowly but clearly.

'It's bin a long time since I 'ad it.' I looked at Mrs Henery for an explanation.

''Es talkin' about that wot yo' cor ate!' she snapped. She sat down in the chair opposite and sighed wearily.

'It's that fancy wench. She's set 'im off agen, strokin' 'is 'ond an' pattin' 'is head 'an 'im gawping saft as shit, the brazen hussy, showing 'er arse an' all! Dun yo' know, when 'er sot theer, where yo' bin,' she leaned forward confidentially and added in a hoarse whisper, 'I sid 'er gusset!'

Hastily I crossed my legs, though I doubted my directoire knickers would rouse any lust in Henery's breast.

'Yo' ring that welfare office, tell 'em never to send 'er again. Bugger the blankets!' she sighed again. 'I'm going t'ave such a game with 'im agen. I'll be wishin' I'd got me hands on 'er ternight!'

139

I didn't say, but it struck me that Henery would be wishing the same thing.

* * *

District nursing is more accommodating for a married nurse with a family and working from home, and naturally I traded under my married name, which was Cockerill. I found it rather an amusing name, the sort you could dine out on, but my sister-in-law had other views. As a child, she said, she had suffered much distress and embarrassment because of it, and when we had children she thought we should change it to protect them.

The whole idea was ludicrous but the seed was sown. How intriguing to choose a new name. I thought longingly of Cholmondely and St John, pronounced Sinjun, and sat up nights reading the telephone directory.

I had almost forgotten the subject when an older colleague whose opinion I valued highly said, 'For heaven's sake, Cocky, why don't you change your name?' (Cocky was my kennel name and still is, though it belies my shy and unassuming nature). The topic was revived, and I even made inquiries as to how it was done. Apparently you can just adopt a name and state you wish to be known by it. It's as simple as that. Alternatively it can be done the hard way by enlisting the services of a solicitor who, after participating in devious spells known only to solicitors, announces your new moniker in the *London Gazette* and, on receipt of £15, hands you your deed poll. The £15 covered the four of us (this was 1952, remember).

When I approached my husband about it, he raised no objection, but stipulated that if it was done it must be done legally and I must do it. My father-in-law was amused but said he certainly didn't mind. My own family were indifferent. It only confirmed what they had always suspected — that I had a tile loose.

Faced with no opposition I lost interest until one day when overtaking my daughter on her way home from school I saw that she was followed by a group of taunting boys. Their licentiousness is best not repeated and my ire soon dispersed them, but when questioned she admitted tearfully that it was a common occurrence. I was inflamed in defence of my young. Soon she was due to move to a new school; she would not go as a Cockerill! While the mood was on me I hastened to phone my father's solicitor and made an appointment for the following day.

That night I lay sleepless, for by morning we had to have a new name. Despite my earlier aspirations I reckoned that one similar to our own would be less complicated and much easier to adopt. Out of the darkness came inspiration: Cotterill. Only two letters needed to be changed, and people might even believe that the other was an error on their part. What was more important, it was a beloved name to perpetuate, a cherished family name reincarnated from the past.

Once more I was at Cotterill's Farm, the ancient home of my father's family and once, for a short period of childhood, mine too. Memories overwhelmed me: the mullioned windows; the old priest-hole where we children played hide-and-seek; Uncle Sim with his tight curly hair slicing mangel-wurzel and surreptitiously slipping me a slice when Mother wasn't looking. Sim, what a grand old family name, smacking of the good earth and medieval husbandry. Sim, I rolled it roung my tongue and loved the flavour of it.

I recalled family Christmases, the roast turning endlessly on the spit, carrots and peas on willow-pattern plates, small boys in knickerbocker suits, hair smarmed back and tongues in cheeks. Little girls with dodging on their drawers and fluted wings of broderie anglaise sprouting from the shoulders of their starched white pinnys. Carols in the parlour with the harsh horse-hair sofa scratching the back of our bare legs, the aunts and uncles glorying in their magnificent voices. Only Uncle George was inharmonious; they shushed him and told him he would put a brass band out.

Then there was Big Jack with his powerful rendering of 'Danny Boy'. Many years later I was to hear him sing the haunting lament for the last time, on the day of his death, as he lay in the old fourposter in which they had all been born. This time it was in a tiny little voice but every note was true.

The farmhouse was a fine Tudor building with modern comforts and capable of housing three families. In 1638 it had been given an outer casing of stone, quarried from nearby, and so bore that date over the great iron-studded oak front door. The front garden was rich with flowers and there was a tennis court on which the family and young folk disported themselves.

After Grandfather's death his fellow councillors, invested with temporary power, decided it was the ideal spot to build their new council estate. 'The farm would made a good museum,' suggested one tentatively. It had been mentioned in local history books as being the most interesting building in the area.

'Who ever would want a museum here?' scoffed the others, though now the Blackcountry Museum is one of the most popular in the country. There was then no law for the protection of old buildings and so the farm was demolished, not without dignity, for the great twisted chimneys defied and broke the tackle brought for their destruction, but now at least the name should be ours.

Having made up my mind I consulted my husband.

Waiting in the solicitor's anteroom I wondered if it would work. I once knew a butcher named Death who changed it to De-ath, but everyone still called him Death. I felt rather foolish; it seemed such a silly thing to have come about.

The solicitor was a kindly man. His avuncular approach invited confidence and I waxed eloquent on the indignity of such a name as ours, the obscenities into which it could be translated by rude little boys, and the utter degradation of it all.

He heard me out and when I had exhausted myself he still sat regarding me across his desk with a quizzical smile.

Then I remembered. His name was Cox.

CHAPTER EIGHT

— Patients and Pets —

MARTHA GAMP WHEN I first beheld her was a benign octogenarian newly scrubbed and released from hospital. She might well have qualified as a candidate when Whistler painted his mum, and it was not until she opened her mouth that she let the cat out of the bag.

She greeted me with an enthusiasm which never flagged during the twelve years I attended her, but her daughters, of whom she had five, she lashed with a vitriolic temper. Ben, her only son, forty and unmarried, alone remained at home and she regarded him with utter contempt. He was a shift-worker and took refuge in his bed. His miserable life was compensated by in incredible ability to sleep, and he was the only man I ever knew who overlay himself when he was on two 'til ten.

That I found favour with Mrs Gamp stemmed from the fact that she had for the greater part of her active life enjoyed the status of a self-appointed midwife and local layer-out, and she regarded me as the medium through which she intended to convey her ancient lore to an ignorant posterity. Since she was a diabetic needing daily insulin, general nursing care and a weekly bath, she had ample time in which to impart her knowledge.

It was customary, except in country areas, for general nurses and midwives to work apart to lessen the risk of infection, but Mrs Gamp deplored this as a lot of bunkum and rejoiced when some complication such as measles in the

143

house or infection in a mother or baby, even flu, necessitated my taking a case over from the midwife. Then she could give me the full benefit of her knowledge.

The mother must be kept on slops for three days, bound firmly with a bolster case and confined to her bed for three weeks, after which everything went 'back with a click'. She must be warned against letting the child glimpse itself in a mirror before its first birthday or, until then, cutting its fingernails; the mother was advised to nibble them, and of course she must never enter another's house until she had been churched. To ensure good eyesight, a spot of urine should be instilled into the infant's eyes, and in the case of girl babies there was an essential ritual known as 'breaking the nipple strings', on which I will not elaborate.

In my routine work, she instructed me on the making of cow-pat poultices (unparalleled for retaining the heat) and 'hungry water', a soap liniment smelling strongly of camphor and foxglove tea. The latter was in great demand for sufferers of bald patches on the scalp; they were instructed to rub it into the afflicted area twice daily and, strangely enough, it was most effective. Not all that strange maybe; digitalis is derived from the foxglove; or maybe the stimulation of the scalp massage contributed to the cure.

Then, of course, there was the all-important technique of laying-out à la Gamp, and the warning that if the corpse was inclined to 'soss', another death in the family was imminent.

Ma Gamp's much maligned daughters were grand women, and though whipped constantly by their mother's virulent tongue they arranged, rota-wise, to cope with her household chores. They were all married, and it was their offspring who were delegated to harvest the herbs in their various seasons. Ma, now unable to negotiate the stairs, occupied the parlour, together with her bed and commode, and all the family trembled in her presence.

Poor Ben suffered from habitual constipation which was not helped by his inactivity. Frequently he was subjected to

enemas saponis, to the disgust of his parent. 'The girt loon!'
she ranted, urging me to lace the soapy water with black
treacle which she maintained would 'agitate 'is guts' and
not only produce the desired result, but would 'gi' 'im sich a
bally airk, 'e wo' niver waent another!'

Ben, though sparse of speech, boasted a colourful vocab-
ulary and, after all, a good cussing does much to lower the
blood pressure. Once, under the misery of a manual
evacuation, he called me a 'Fuckin' lousebound bastard',
and though later, when relieved, he said shamefacedly: 'I
day mane it, nus,' I was stirred by the sheer poetry of the
epithet and for a long time after, when having to sign my
name, to SRN I added FLB. Nobody ever questioned it.
Perhaps, like the story of the king in the altogether, they
hesitated to air their ignorance.

Ma Gamp, daily anticipating her demise, dictated to us
all as to the disposal of her cadaver. Cremation was
definitely off. 'If yo' bern me I'll ornt yer!' she threatened.
'I'm agooin' up Ockabonk, in the cherchyard on top o' yer
ferther.' She cackled evilly: 'That'll shairk 'im, me on top!'

Her daughters, discomforted, avoided each other's gaze
and shushed the children out to play on the 'fo'd'. If she
began reminiscing, there was no knowing what might be
revealed.

One morning, towards midday, I was attending another
patient in the vicinity when a neighbour of the Gamps'
arrived. 'See o'd Martha's gone at last,' she volunteered.

'Never!' I cried. 'She was lively enough when I was there a
couple of hours ago!'

'Well 'er doh look very lively now,' ejaculated the
woman, and went on to describe how, on seeing the curtains
drawn, she had investigated and found Martha dead. She
had roused Ben and despatched him to summon the rest of
the family.

She regarded me quizzically. ''Er'd bin layed owt a treat.
If yo' day dew it, 'ew did?'

Perplexed, I hurried off to investigate. As she stated, the
curtains were drawn, and in the darkened room the family

stood surveying the sheeted form on the bed.

'P'raps it's for the best,' they said with ill-concealed relief.

'Thank God!' came from a more outspoken son-in-law.

Reverently I turned back the sheet revealing the aged face, the jaw expertly bound with a large white hankerchief, the eyelids weighted with the traditional pennies. One penny slipped eschew, a hoary eye gazed into mine, and the corpse, struggling with its trappings croaked: 'Lift me up, nus. I wanta piddle.'

Two daughters rushed shrieking into the street, one fainted clean away, another began to have hysterics. Ben was the first to recover. 'Strewth!' he breathed. 'I goo ter the bottom of ower stairs!'

Mrs Gamp was unabashed. Now enthroned upon her commode, she hugged herself. 'Med a good job o' mesen, day I, nus? As fer yo' buggers,' she addressed the remnants of her family, 'cotched yo' lot proper, day I? 'Agglin' over me divi' afore I'm co'd! Nor yer wo' git me 'surance book neether, I'n bernt it!'

'Doh knock en!' cried the long suffering son-in-law. 'When time does cum tha' wo' be left above ground, not if I 'as ter bury yer meself!'

When time did come it was peacefully in her sleep at the age of ninety-two. With my last job for her completed, she lay serene and strangely quiescent, her eyelids in repose without the need of pennies. Her silver hair, bound with my daughter's white ribbons, shone like a halo.

The family eyed her warily and, fearful of another resurrection, begged me to attend the funeral. To be on the safe side they kept her for two weeks before burial.

Fortunately the weather was cold.

* * *

I had an arduous job, a husband and two young children, and it was irresponsible of me to want a dog as well but I did, so we thought about it and that was the first step. The second step was to fence the garden securely. It was good strong fencing but that was an investment anyway where gardens and toddlers are concerned.

Then GL saw an advertisement in the evening paper: a litter of whippets for sale, 7 guineas each, too pricey for us, but ever since Melody had charmed me with grace of movement and come-hither eyes I had yearned for a whippet, and so the breed was selected too. A few weeks later a further advertisement for a single whippet at the same kennels but for £2 intrigued us. 'Wonder what's wrong with it?' we thought simultaneously until our days off coincided, and then we decided to find out.

It was a time-consuming trip necessitating three buses but a day out together was always call for excitement and Judy was old enough to take notice and share in the adventure. We had come prepared with one of her discarded cot blankets, the blue woolly one which had been my first purchase for her. Now it was our homecoming gift for the pup, unless of course he had already been sold. He hadn't and the owner of the kennels seemed grimly anxious that he should be. She left us sitting on a chintz-covered couch in a room reminiscent of many breeders I had known, untidily elegant and smelling of dogs. In a few moments she returned carrying a lanky little pup, older than I had expected, and set him down before us. His name, she announced pompously, was Aladdin's Lamp. Sacrilegiously we giggled and she was not amused.

The strange coltish little creature did nothing to fulfil the picture conjured up by the cuddlesome word puppy. Everything about him was awkward and elongated: his spindly legs, his rat-like tail, his long inquiring nose. GL looked dubious and I felt I had let the side down by lauding so lavishly the wonder of whippets.

'Must get rid of him,' the woman was saying. 'Off to America for twelve months. Have breeder friend who will accommodate my bitches while I'm away, but not a dog of course, no dogs.' She shook her head and her pursed lips condemned the male sex in general. 'Rest of litter sold like hot cakes, can't understand it, nobody wants him.'

Sensing our hesitation she brought the price down to

thirty bob, but she had no need. She had already sold him, for the words 'Nobody wants him' had made him the most desirable puppy in the world.

I scooped him up into the blue blanket but it failed to contain him entirely; however meticulously he was wrapped there was always a dangling leg or long, long tail hanging out from somewhere and an excited twitching nose exploring the alien aroma of my neck. Triumphantly I bore him away, leaving GL to cope with the cash and our larger bundle of offspring.

Rich with our new possession we negotiated the three buses home. Fellow passengers beamed, making indulgent clucking noises to which the pup responded with ecstatic whinnyings. Judy, anxious to share the attention, emulated him.

When at last we turned the corner of our street Elizabeth, already home from school, was swinging on the garden gate impatient for our return. 'Let me see it! Let me see it!' she cried, her mouth full of bread and jam, as I marched into the house and deposited the blue bundle on the hearth rug. We all watched breathlessly as the puppy extricated himself. Father, who had been holding the fort, scratched his white head and the little dog was revealed in all his gawkiness. There was a pregnant silence. Elizabeth finished her bread and jam.

'What will it grow up to be?' she asked doubtfully.

With large anxious eyes the pup surveyed us, strangers on whom his whole life and well-being now depended. Eager to please he watched the mouths, their expression was kindly but mouths, he knew, could change to become cruel, scolding, berating his misdemeanours and lashing him with harsh words. These, he decided, approved him; he rose on to his spindly legs and wagged his whole rear so vigorously that he fell over again. Encouraged by the laughter his performance engendered he got up and pirouetted, mouthing his haunches and chasing his own lengthy tail, then impelled by a sudden urge he squatted and made a puddle. The mouths changed, showing disapproval; hands seized him and bore him away in the midst of his micturition so that he trailed wee throughout the house.

Dumped in the garden, his attention was diverted from the calls of nature by an errant leaf which he chased until a flurry of rain penetrated his fine coat and sent him scurrying for the house. Drawn to the warmth of the hearth, he found a dish of food and a bowl of water upon a tablecloth of newspapers. Excited by the rustle of paper he seized a corner and worried it with immature growls, tearing it to shreds and shedding food and water into a disorganized mess. The mouths again shown consternation; hands dealt with the débâcle and food was once more placed before him. This time he devoured it voraciously.

After another session in the garden and wearied by all the strange happenings he explored the room, instinctively seeking some sanctum for himself. The basket provided, virtuously scoured with disinfectant, he rejected with a twitch of his elegant proboscis, choosing instead a fat armchair plump with cushions and low enough for him to scrabble into. Impelled by some primeval impulse he turned round several times before settling down and making it his own.

While he slept we tackled the all-important problem of choosing a name, not a decision to be trifled with. Monikers are of great personal consequence, for if they ridicule, or can be so diverted, they are a stigma to be borne for life and often the unhappy bearer is driven to conform with the wretched title.

Aladdin was out but we tore it apart in search of abbreviations. Ali? Laddie? No, too mundane for so original a hound. We discarded his registered name and set off afresh. I favoured Punch, in keeping with his long nose, but could that be ridicule again? Anyway Punch and Judy? The pup slept fitfully, oblivious to the momentous discussion in progress. He made little sucking sounds and his legs jerked convulsively as though he was running a great race. We gathered around and stared at him in search of inspiration. Then Elizabeth suggested Bo'sun; the Dales of diary fame had a Bo'sun she informed us, and we considered it. The name had a certain dignity and a nautical flavour which complimented GL and so we settled for it. Elizabeth, delighted by her success, brought out my best cut-glass sugar bowl filled with water. Delicately she sprinkled a few drops on his silken head.

'I name thee Bo'sun, she announced solemnly.

Bo'sun twitched spasmodically and in his dreams ran faster than ever.

*   *   *

Sometime during the night the little dog woke to find himself alone. Darkness held no terrors for him; when in the beginning he had been created out of a warm darkness filled with love and sustenance and constant movement, he knew no personal shape and was conscious only of being a mouth groping for a teat. Later from the squirming mass he had emerged as an individual but never had he been alone. Now in this strange place terror assailed him; out of despair and isolation he raised his head and keened as only a whippet can.

I woke immediately and recognized the sound. Fearful that the family might be disturbed, I hurried to him. He sat so desolate, so little-dog-lost that I hugged him to me with idiotic endearments and he reciprocated with effusive slobbering. Poor little creature, why he was cold! I warmed some milk and while he was lapping it up I unearthed one of Judy's discarded baby vests. With his front legs through the sleeves and a piece cut out to accommodate his shushy it was just the thing. Having resettled him in his chair I returned to bed, but I was only halfway upstairs when the whining followed me with renewed vigour and it was accompanied by frantic scratching on the door. Hastily I returned but not this time with idiotic twaddle. He fled from my menacing mouth, whimpering, tail between legs. Relenting I comforted him and added a cardigan to the little vest, but the performance was repeated every time he was left. Of course I knew the solution – take him to bed with me

– I'd been had that way before!

I compromised and spent the rest of the night sharing his chair.

*　*　*

My husband enjoyed shopping and since he was on shift-work had every opportunity for doing it, which was most convenient for me. He became a familiar figure pushing the large pram with Judith sitting at one end and Bo'sun at the other. Bo'sun became so addicted to this method of transport that when Judith outgrew her perambulator he never quite recovered from the loss of his conveyance until we had a car. After the initial indignities of being wormed and inoculated he had become an important member of the family and was developing into a very elegant little dog much loved by us all.

Meanwhile Judith had become a real 'bossy boots'. She was very tiny, dark-haired, dark-eyed with a golden brown skin. 'Nothing but a little brown nut!' cried one of my patients on first seeing her, but she was full of her own importance. One day when all of my in-laws were staying with us she burst into the room crying:

'Do you know, no one in this house has had their bowels moved today! I marked the toilet roll this morning and it hasn't moved an inch!'

She had such an excess of energy that we were all exhausted and decided that at a very early age she should go to dancing school to wear herself out, but she was indefatigable and we only wore ourselves out taking and fetching her. What a rod we had made for our backs (and a hole for our pockets!). Now began the era of tutus, greasepaint and sequins as she danced her way through endless shows and pantomimes put on for various charities. Judith was just six when she danced her first solo ballet at the Hippodrome – and she was hooked.

*　*　*

Although she was becoming rather dunny and more

decrepit in body Mrs Tibbs was far more alert in mind; television had re-educated her.

It all began with the Coronation. Mrs Tibbs loved the new Queen with a deep, abiding devotion and she was determined to see her crowned. Television was in its infancy but a set could be had for a short trial period of time – time enough to view the ceremony. Since she was housebound Mrs Buggins from next door was her informant on these intricacies and so was invited to share her viewing and to perform other small services.

Buggins was an unassuming little woman, slow and fumbling but with the use of her legs, which was what Mrs Tibbs lacked. Together they made one functional body so Mrs Buggins shopped around and would trudge a mile to save a penny. Shopkeepers knew her and she had priority for broken biscuits, over-ripe bananas and squashed cream cakes; it all saved chewing and neither had a surfeit of gnashers and the two rejoiced together over each small economy, surreptitiously hoarding titbits for the great day, preparatory to which Mrs Buggins was cleaning the windows.

'Doh clean th'outside,' admonished Mrs Tibbs. 'We doh want everybody gawpin' in, just clean th'inside so as we can see out.'

She herself was arranging her vast collection of royal photographs on the chiffonier. They were dominated by the tinted one of Princess May of Teck inscribed with her full name – Victoria Mary Augusta Louise Olga Pauline Claudine Agnes.

That tiny-waisted girl had become Queen Mary and Mrs Tibbs's pulse quickened to think that she would soon be seeing her grandaughter's coronation.

She woke the next morning with a feeling of excitement and remembered – it was Coronation Day. In the darkness the window became a paler shade of grey and she fumbled under the pillow for her torch. The fingers of the clock on her bedside chair showed fifteen minutes past midnight but it only went upside down so she reckoned that made it a quarter to seven, time to get up. She felt down the bed for her rolling pin which lay alongside her; she nightly anticipated rape and went to bed well prepared to defend her virtue. With it she thumped the wall and there was an answering thud. Buggins too was awake.

By telly-time they had the hearth swept, the ashes riddled and the salvaged gleeds ready to bank the fire with during the lengthy entertainment, for it was parky and rain spattered on the window pane. They breakfasted on toast rich with good beef dripping and well sprinkled with pepper, and added a drop of 'old crater' to enhance their cups of tea. The Groaty Dick they planned to feast on, when the Royals were having their banquet, was already prepared. It was a pity about the weather.

Mrs Tibbs wore her best black alpaca and even Buggins had a new pinny, but when the Queen appeared in all her glory she looked so radiant they felt they could well do without the sun.

When the National Anthem was played Mrs Tibbs tottered tremulously on to her rotting old appendages; she knew her duty if Buggins didn't. The royal coach had just arrived at the Abbey and the Queen looked straight at her, smiling and raising a hand in salute. Mrs Tibbs bobbed deferentially and waved back.

"Er sid me! 'Er sid me!' she rejoiced, flopping back into her chair.

'Then 'old yer 'ush!' admonished Buggins. 'Or 'er'll 'ear yer as well.' But the Queen had moved on into the Abbey and showed no sign of having heard.

Suddenly they too were in the Abbey, bemused by the strange music and awed with the wonder of it all, and when the Queen was finally crowned she looked so young and small to bear so heavy a burden that they snivelled surreptitiously. Later, during the return procession down the aisle, there was a moment when her face was full of wonder, as though she had escaped the multitudes and been alone to some secret place.

Then the bells began to ring and the cannons to boom and

the people to cheer and the rain to bedew high and low alike.

It took the two old ladies some time to recover from their experience. Buggins was the first to come down to earth.

'Well,' she said thoughtfully, 'I expect 'er's just the same as we bin underneath all them tranklements.'

'Then it's God 'elp Philip!' cried Mrs Tibbs fervently.

*   *   *

Of course there was no going back; after the Coronation they were hooked. The telly man, who had the savvy to know that the elderly and housebound would be his most enthusiastic viewers, agreed to rent his cheaper sets to old-age pensioners without the advance sum usually demanded. Rent included maintenance which was a big item and Madams Tibbs and Buggins were delighted with the arrangement.

The pattern of their lives changed to give priority to viewing times for they watched everything. They became experts on racing, reviled politicians to their faces, and celebrities became their personal friends. It was in the days of the epilogue, and they enjoyed that; it saved them saying their prayers. It was nice too to say 'Goodnight' to the Queen, though as Mrs Tibbs said, 'It's a cryin' shame the way they keep that poor wench up 'til all hours with 'er crown on.'

Because of her increasing infirmities I had been able to get a free home help allocated for Mrs Tibbs but the supervisor was hard put to accommodate her, for she waged constant war on the ladies and many departed in distress, refusing ever to do for her again. Miss Price, the latest recruit, was a maiden lady of tact and determination. She pursued her tasks with a one-track mind and a deaf ear and for a while peace reigned, but of course it couldn't last. Mrs Tibbs began accusing her of filching some of her allotted time in order to spend longer with Mr Cutt two doors away.

'Anythin' to get a mon!' she reviled and made lewd insinuations, though the fact that Mr Cutt was ninety-four hardly made him eligible for what she had in mind.

Finally she refused to sign Miss Price's time-sheet. It was the last straw and once more the supervisor's help was enlisted. This time she would stand no nonsense.

'I'm sorry, Mrs Tibbs,' she said firmly, 'but I shall have to cut Miss Price's time to one hour only.'

'Daze yer 'ide!' cried Mrs Tibbs outraged. 'Why 'er's in and out now like a bloody fart in a colander!'

The supervisor departed in high dudgeon.

'Sod 'er!' said Mrs Tibbs, unrepentant.

After this I suggested that Mrs Buggins should be given the Good Neighbour's allowance in lieu of a home help, and the idea was accepted with alacrity and with equal joy by Mrs Tibbs and Buggins, for the allowance was more than enough to pay the telly rent and Buggins would only be doing what she'd done before anyway.

The tenor of their lives moved smoothly, lulled by the magic of television.

* * *

One of the nicest things about gardening is that if you put it off long enough it's eventually too late. We were never gardeners so when it was too late for us we bought tons of broken slabs and hid our shortcomings under a patio on which we assembled a conglomeration of tubs, stone troughs and earthenware pots. In these vessels I planted geraniums and colourful flowers that were obtained from a local nursery. A sneaky instant mode of gardening but effective, and to add to the authenticity Father had planted some of his flowering shrubs at the bottom of our patch which made an attractive background to the patio.

In the beginning, fired with enthusiasm, we had bought an apple tree, a Cox's Orange Pippin, for Gun-layer dearly loved to eat an apple straight from the tree, but the years had passed without it even producing any bloom.

One day Mrs Tibbs, who was fancying 'a bit of the green stuff', suggested I might like to bring her some lettuce from our garden. She was astounded to find that we didn't grow anything edible.

'Anybody with a husband and a bit of sod can grow lettuce,' she remarked sourly, and spurred on by her disapproval I bought a packet of lettuce seed and sowed it carefully in the shadow of the shrubs. Mrs Tibbs didn't let me forget. She brought a text from her bedroom and hung it over the mantle shelf where I would see it every day and hopefully improve my ways. It read:

> Whoever plants a seed beneath the sod
> And waits for it to turn aside the clod –
> He trusts in God.

I waited for it to turn aside the clod and to my surprise and delight it did. Tiny green shoots pricked the earth and quickly grew in great profusion. The instructions on the packet told me I must thin them out but I was loth to do so for it smacked of infanticide to me, and when the over-crowding compelled me to I replanted the little rejects, but they only withered and died. However the others flourished and I tended them like a mother.

One morning as I was preparing his breakfast GL called excitedly from the garden. He was gazing ecstatically at the apple tree and behold it bore one single spray of beautiful pink blossom. We hugged each other joyfully, visualizing the delicious Cox's Orange Pippins it would become. I too had a success to disclose. I led him to the lettuce which had now grown big enough to be recognizable but Clem, our tortoise, had got there first. He was just crunching up the last one.

I did what I should have done at the beginning. I went to the greengrocer's and bought the biggest lettuce I could find. When I gave it to Mrs Tibbs she didn't ask from whence it came; she was too busy telling me how easy it was to grow tomatoes.

Judith was already home from school when I returned, her eyes shining with anticipation. 'O Mom,' she cried, 'I've found something lovely for you, you'll never guess. Now shut your eyes,' she commanded and led me into the lounge. 'Now open them.'

I did and there, on the table, in my number one vase, displayed to its best advantage, was the spray of pink apple blossom.

*   *   *

Old Eli dwelt in a corner of the house-top under the eaves, well away from the wide house which was really his and from the brawling woman who was his daughter-in-law. It is soul-destroying to be old and unwanted, and he waited hopefully to be rehoused in a home for the aged. He was a mild little man, but the meek are not always blessed and his contemporaries on the waiting list who were less quiescent potched him every time.

The brawling woman commandeered his pension to pay for his miserable gas fire and the fodder she begrudgingly doled out for him, and I attended to give him a weekly blanket bath and injections for the anaemia which was not improved by the aforesaid fodder.

In the yard a very off-putting mongrel trailed its chain through the putrefying accumulation of its own excreta and responded to my overtures of friendship with a savage snarl and a menacing curl of the upper lip. I had always before been able to win over the most belligerent of *canis familiaris* but I never trust one that is tethered, for the strength of a chain lies in its weakest link and one day that link will surely sever.

When I broached the subject of the dog to Eli's daughter-in-law she snorted that the creature had never been loose; only her husband dared to approach it and then armed with a goad. Poor brute! No wonder it waged a vendetta with *homo sapiens*.

There was also a scrawny cat, munched and scarred and lumpy with kittens. One day it was keening sadly, its progeny gone. 'In bucket!' bellucked the woman, 'same as t'others!' and later I found the cat in a corner of Eli's garret mewling over one of his knotted old socks and proffering dugs rich with wasted milk. The next time it was pregnant I asked if one could be saved for me; the cat should have some

157

joy in its barren life and maybe in future I could canvas for homes to save one from each litter. Out of her very meanness the brawling woman balked, so I offered to take on the job of emptying Eli's commode to appease her.

When the births were imminent I provided a box lined with woollies. The woman would not tolerate it in the house but I established it in a corner of the large outside loo and baited it with titbits brought from home so that the cat accepted it. I was rewarded, for one morning she lay suckling a solitary kitten and the warm brown sound of purring was a hymn of thanksgiving.

She knew three weeks of fulfilment and then it happened. I had just emptied Eli's commode in the closet when the weakest link snapped and the dog hurtled in. I tried to keep Eli's receptacle between us, and the brawling woman had perfidiously slammed shut the back door with herself on the safe side of it, when the cat with an unearthly scream landed on the dog's head. In the ensuing mayhem I rescued the kitten and tucked it in the bodice of my dress, but when the unfortunate hound hared down the road never to return, the poor broken body of the cat lay dead upon the fold.

I didn't reproach the woman for infidelity but humbly, for I feared a refusal, asked for the kitten. The family were delighted with the new acquisition. We fed the tiny bumbling creature with milk from a doll's bottle and soft red pulp scraped from the surface of raw beef, and we bedded it with Bo'sun who brooded over it with loving care and croodled the little orphan within the circle of his long body, cleansing it meticulously.

When it was grown into a lordly tom it reciprocated by warming his old bones on winter nights.

*   *   *

It is inevitable that one becomes involved with the animals of a house when frequenting it. Sometimes when there was a litter of pups I was compromised into docking their tails if the breed demanded that mutilation. Remembering Cloggy, a familiar of my schooldays, it seemed kinder to do it than to leave it to some hamfisted Tom, Dick or Harry who might botch the job.

Cloggy was as sinister a character as you could hope to meet in a month of Sundays and he lived with a witch. She might have been his mother or even his wife. Cloggy was of indeterminate age, but certainly the old gammer was a witch for she was wall-eyed and toothless and her curved beak and upturned chin almost met. In their backyard a long-handled birch broom leaned drunkenly against the wall, obviously for nocturnal transport, and as we passed en route for school we crossed our fingers and spat over them as a proviso against the occult.

Cloggy himself was a Pied Piper who drew children magnetically in his wake, for he was an odd job man with a bent for the macabre. He dug graves and cesspits, disposed of rejected pets, wrung the necks of chickens destined for the pot and docked puppy dogs' tails. He was a familiar figure trailing a reluctant dog on a string in the direction of the canal, an ominous brick in his hand.

Our classroom window was purposely designed to thwart the wandering eye but Cloggy had a gammy leg and his ungainly gait, accentuated by hobnailed boots, identified him, so that when he passed we stirred resentfully, speculating on where he might be going without us. Our teacher, 'Catty-white-drawers', who also recognized the 'hoppity-hop', would rap smartly for attention.

There was an outcry recently on the radio against tail docking, and the radio campaigner converted me. I am a sucker for conversion, changing my religion and politics at the drop of a hat, and all the tiny tails which I have nipped off with clippers, applying a swab of Friar's Balsam to the sad little stump, hang heavily on my conscience.

Cloggy was less clinical. The word soon got around if any local bitch had whelped and unless it was of a long-tailed breed we knew the gruesome ritual would be enacted. Cloggy worked better with an audience and would ivver-ovver until there was a suitable assemblage. We responded by making a feast of the performance and congregated with such sustenance as tiger nuts, bull's eyes, gobstoppers and long brown locus beans, the sweet pod of the carob and resembling dried banana skins but really quite delicious.

When all was hushed and still, except for a satisfactory sucking and the frequent inspection of gobstoppers which underwent many colour changes before reaching the tiny seed in the centre, Cloggy commenced. Then all sucking ceased and our toes curled in horrific anticipation.

Selecting one of the unfortunate pups laid sacrificially before him Cloggy would put the tiny creature to his mouth and manipulate the minute vertebra of its tail between his teeth. The hapless pup scriggled in vain, there was a scrunch, an agonized shriek, and yammering grievously it was discarded for the next victim, while the boys jostled for the tail spat out by Cloggy and the girls recoiled with feminine delicacy.

When the executions were over Cloggy would clear his throat raspingly, eject a gob of phlegm and then, delicately taking his nostrils between thumb and forefinger (and diplomatically turning his back to the wind), would blow his nose in the gutter.

The mother of the litter was secured at the onset but on one occasion the bitch, a sharp little terrier, broke loose just as he was operating on one of her offspring and Cloggy, being rather dunny, didn't hear her coming until she sank her teeth into his unwary buttock. His sharp intake of breath was calamitous, for the tail he had just bitten off went down the wrong way and despite much hawking and wambling and thumping on the back it refused to be dislodged.

The effect on Cloggy was traumatic. He never performed again with the same aplomb and soon joined the fraternity of the night-soil men which conveniently put him on the same shift as his witch.

*　　*　　*

Mrs Wilks was not my patient so the story is not truly mine, but my informant doesn't mind the repetition.

Mrs Wilks's doctor was not satisfied with her condition so he decided on a second opinion and the consultant agreed on a domiciliary visit. The old lady lived alone and, as was customary, the two doctors took a nurse with them as chaperone. On arrival at the cottage they all had a little chat to put the patient at her ease before the consultant prepared to make his examination. Then he said:

'Now, dear, will you get undressed, please?' There was no response from Mrs Wilks.

'Come, dear, take your knickers off, there's a good girl.' There was still no response so his tone became a little impatient.

'Come on, dear, get your clothes off. Can you hear me, Mrs Wilks?'

Mrs Wilks replied: 'O yes, I can 'ear yer, Doctor, but I thought you was talkin' to the nurse!'

CHAPTER NINE

— On the District —

HAD IT BEEN left to my husband I would never have learned to drive, for he abhorred lady drivers and most of all resented my having access to our wonderful new possession – a shining new Morris Minor. When I took a course of lessons at a driving school that didn't disturb him – it was their car – but my practising on our own caused real physical suffering and he went into a spasm every time I crashed the gears. I would never have mastered it had it not been for the patience and determination of Joe, a doughty neighbour and friend of ours, though GL magnanimously decided to give me an hour's tuition immediately before my driving test. Nothing could have done more to undermine my confidence – after twenty minutes I insisted on waiting at the place of my appointment to recover my equilibrium.

I resolved to put this first test down to experience and when the examiner got into the car a calm descended upon me. I was not wearing uniform in case someone accused me of currying favour, and wore an unprepossessing old mackintosh for the rain was torrential.

Gun-layer was waiting for our return. 'Move over,' he said, coming to the driving seat when the examiner had gone. Then he saw the slip of paper in my hand. 'You haven't passed?' he cried in horror as I grinned up at him, but he wouldn't let me drive. 'You'll be too excited,' he complained, and I never drove that dear little car again for he took it straight to the garage from whence it had come.

'We'll trade it in,' he said, making it sound like a favour, 'before you knock it about. It's really too small for us anyway.' He was certainly right there.

Seeing me still plodding the beat few people believed that I had passed my test. It was some weeks before our new car came and when it did it was a much larger car, a Morris Cowley, and the gears were on the steering column. Technically I'm a write-off and my husband happily believed that I would never master the gears, accomplished motorists had been known to fall foul of this new mechanical device, but it so happened that when the car came I was just having some overdue leave. The intrepid Peg, thus lumbered with my extra work, agreed to let me chauffeur her round the district and with her moral support and my own determination we became conversant with the dratted gears.

Back on duty it was with a feeling of exhilaration that I set off each morning in my chariot. After years of hoofing it, heavy-laden like a camel, this was emancipation!

Bo'sun, sitting aloof and proud beside me all day, except for an occasional run on waste ground, had come into his own.

* * *

As usual Christmas had caught me napping. Every year I resolved that I would shop in October and write cards in November, leaving me free for the exigencies of December, but I am an improvident creature and never learn by experience. Hospitals plan a general exodus at this time and discharge patients prematurely, while long-term institutions just let them loose for the festive period. This influx of patients still needing nursing care is one of the burdens of Christmas for the district nurse, and on the day itself essential treatment and care of the very ill must still be carried out.

The day before Christmas Eve I had a call from the nursing superviser (our Queen Bee) to alert me that the nurse on my adjoining area had gone sick and would I do her relief. It wasn't a question but a command and I was furious. Why me? (Because you were the first one she could cop on the phone, you fool!) As an administrator she was off-duty herself by now and only anxious to pass the buck. In vain I protested, pleading overwork myself, we too had a staff shortage; it all fell on deaf ears. 'You get too involved with your own patients, nurse. You must cut down there,' she answered coldly, putting down the phone.

Troubles never come singly and during the day the car broke down. This was calamitous, in fact outrageous, for it was almost new and I couldn't possibly manage without it. I phoned the garage from whence it had come. Propitiously they agreed to deal with it though warning me that they closed at midday on Christmas Eve, so it must be collected between eleven-thirty and twelve o'clock or I would be without it all over the holiday. Sometimes I thought it would be better not to have a car, for then your limitations were recognized, whereas with a car you were expected to move mountains, and when the wretched vehicle let you down you were still lumbered with the mountain.

The following day, Christmas Eve, I set off very early on foot and hampered with a light raincoat which I could pop over my uniform when I went to fetch the car. I couldn't face Dudley in the conspicuity of my uniform and I certainly wouldn't have time to go home and change, apart from which we were not expected to leave our beat while on duty. I planned to conduct my transformation at Mrs Tibbs; she was used to my vagaries and accepted them resignedly but not without curiosity.

'Wheer bin yo gooin'?' she demanded as I executed the quick change, and when I explained, she said:

'Then while yo'm theer get me money back on this.'

Blatantly ignoring my protests she brought forth a cardigan still encased in its cellophane wrapping. She was always getting her home help to make purchases for her at a certain store, then a few weeks later she would badger me to return the dratted things and get her money back. I hate asking for refunds but it was a service the shop granted without demur so I usually complied on my day off. But now of all times!

She put the garment into its original bag and thrust it on me. 'I want the money fer me turkey,' she whined, and remembering it would probably be reduced in the after Christmas sale I took it, cursing myself for not having changed elsewhere. I might have known she would turn it to her own advantage. Leaving my hat and nursing bag with her I made for the bus.

En route for the garage I decided to get rid of Mrs Tibbs's parcel first. The store was crowded with Christmas shoppers and as I pushed through the swing doors hot air engulfed me and I was drawn like a helpless swimmer into a whirlpool of humanity. Desperately I surfaced and fought my way to the appropriate counter where a queue waited. When my turn came and I handed over the garment I noticed the price was still on, just over four pounds. The girl after a deft examination of it gave me a chit for five, but when I drew her attention to the discrepancy she rebuked me.

'It's gone up since then, and we always refund the current price. Kindly move on,' and propelled by the basket of the woman behind I moved. That old faggot Mrs Tibbs! However had she cottoned on to this lark of waiting to get her refund when the price would have gone up? One day it would have gone down and then she'd have a shock. I was at the customer service desk in another queue when I realized the time. I ought to have collected the car first, but then I would never have found anywhere to park it. At last I changed my chit for a crisp fiver which I folded and put in my left-hand pocket carefully. I would keep my own money in the right. I was making for the swing doors when I froze. Coming through them was the Queen Bee herself.

'Don't panic,' I told myself sternly. 'Quick! Get behind that clothes rack.' Colourful contraptions concealed me, but what if I was revealed? Shopping when I should be on duty, especially after prating so about being overworked. I could have explained the car but not Mrs Tibbs.

'You must not get so involved with your own patients,

nurse.' How right she was and she was coming nearer. I snatched a bright pink satin blouse off the rack and held it up before my face as though inspecting it; later when peering cautiously round it I saw her proceeding upstairs to the lingerie. I made a dash for the doors, impeded all the way, and then I had some difficulty getting through. With a sense of guilt I realized that in my haste I had pushed aside a heavily pregnant girl and with apologies I stepped back and held the door ajar for her. It was then I saw what had hindered my progress. I was still holding the pink satin blouse! As I stared at it in horror a hand gripped my shoulder and I shrank from the condemning countenance of what was obviously the store detective.

No! Never! This couldn't happen to me!

I felt sick and faint and unable to defend myself. The shop whirled and my knees had no substance.

'I didn't do it!' I bleated nauseously but the detective's lip curled and a crowd gathered sensing a kill (and where was the Queen Bee now?). I visualized the headlines: 'Nurse caught shoplifting.' Gun-layer would never forgive me – and what about my family?

'Please God get me out of this! I will be good. You know I never pinch anything – well, perhaps a bit of white lint here and there – and that baby cream from the clinic to rub on my hands – everybody does – I'll take it back, I promise – *Please* God!'

The pregnant girl had come forward and challenged my captor.

'Yo' cor charge 'er, 'ers inside the doors.'

'She wasn't, and still has one foot outside.'

'Yo've got t'ave both outside.'

The pregnant one obviously knew her rights. She turned to me. 'I'll come ter court with yer.' Court! Good heavens!

The crowds were joining in with seasonal good humour. 'Goo on, give the wench a break! It's Christmas.' Jocularly they bunted the detective. 'Strewth! 'ers started!'

My pregnant friend had suddenly bent two-double, clutching her belly and emitting an agonized 'Moo.'

For the first time the store detective's face took on a human expression: it registered horror.

'Get out! Both of you!' and snatching the blouse from me, 'I must admit I never knew anyone take one on a hanger before!'

Outside on the pavement, still supporting the girl, I became articulate again, pouring out my relief and gratitude, but she would have none of it.

'Gotta stick together, aye we?' she grinned. She was making a remarkable recovery but the least I could do was offer her a lift home. I explained about the car and the urgent need to collect it.

'Then I'll wait for yer,' she said. 'Over theer, by the WC,' and she indicated the public convenience over the road. I rushed off gutterwise to avoid the crowded pavements and only just made it. The garage was about to close for Christmas but the car was waiting and roadworthy once more. Behind the wheel I felt secure again, as though I had awakened from a nightmare, and in a long cavalcade of traffic, bumper to bumper, I made slow progress back through the town, light-headed and buoyant with relief.

'What about me?' nudged God at my elbow.

'Bless you, God, and thank you. I won't forget.'

When I drew alongside the loo my friend was just coming up the steps. She was as flat as a pancake and carrying two bulging shopping bags which had been empty before. Blithely ignoring the toots of irate drivers she nipped across the road and slumped thankfully into the seat beside me. The tent-like coat hung open now, revealing a long knitted tubular garment which hung flatly about her lean body like a deflated balloon. The shopping bags which she'd plonked between her legs disclosed a multitude of unwrapped very new garments.

'Whatever will you do with all those?' I gasped, easing back into the traffic.

'Why get the money back on 'em at the West Bromwich an' Brummagem stores!' she laughed.

'Now if I were you,' I advised knowledgeably, 'I should

hang on to them for a bit. They're sure to go up in price before long.'

Mrs Tibbs was delighted with the five pound notes I gave her.

The crisp fiver had disappeared into thin air.

*　　*　　*

Some of the houses still defying demolition had been built to house the prolific Victorians. Poker-faced façades over-looked narrow streets and back entrances opened onto a communal yard, the playground of innumerable children and commonly known as the fold. Such a building housed the Finnegans. The family consisted of Ma and Pa, nine assorted offspring, Grandma Finnegan and a widowed uncle known as Gaffer. Grandma was stone deaf. Hearing aids were quite ineffectual; no sound pierced her silent world and I think she appreciated the protection her deafness provided. She smiled and nodded and obligingly buttered endless 'pieces' for her grandchildren.

Gaffer was the original tenant; years ago on the death of his wife his niece had moved in to do for him. When she later became espoused to the fertile Finnegan it was taken for granted that her husband and mother-in-law should move in too. Gaffer, however, clung with the tenacity of the aged to his rent book and one day he told me how he first came by it.

He was, he said, a young masher out walking with his girl when they passed the house, which had been recently vacated. Houses were two a penny with even a rent-free week for scrubbing it out.

'We'll 'ave that,' he joked, pointing to the empty house.

'Do yer mean it?' she asked.

'Arr,' he laughed, and thought no more of it.

When they met the following night she said, 'We con 'ave it.'

''Ave wot?' he asked mystified.

'That 'ouse, yer fule!'

She had had his name put in the rent book. Come Sunday

the banns were read and before he knew it he was wed. Now his rent book warded off the shadow of the workhouse and he slept with it under his pillow.

After each succeeding pregnancy Ma Finnegan had complications with her bosom. This is where I came in but now she had been sterilized and the offending bosom 'took off'. The last baby, a son rejoicing in the name of Garth, was a puny child, quite unlike his namesake, a superman who romped cartoon-wise through the pages of a popular daily, but he survived.

Although Ma no longer needed my ministrations there was nearly always someone in the family who did and now poor Gaffer was getting trouble with his waterworks.

'Let's see,' I said when writing my report and consulting the newspaper which did double duty as a tablecloth. 'It's the fourth today isn't it?'

'Arr!' grieved Ma. 'Our Garth musta bin five yesterday. Aye it a shame, 'e day 'arf 'ave a lampin'!' With a rush of maternal affection she clutched the bewildered child to her remaining bosom and wiped his snotty nose on her apron.

The next day I took a few discarded toys for Garth but he was gone. His fifth birthday, belatedly remembered, was a milestone and he had been dispatched with his brothers and sisters to school.

The Finnegans qualified for free dinners. The next day I asked Ma how he had got on at school.

'God a'mighty!' she shrieked. 'Yo' oughta see 'im! 'E doh 'arf think 'es somebody now. Why 'e come 'ome yesterday – wanted 'is tea off a plate!'

*   *   *

Jeremy was an only child, an overprotected child, for he was the sole product of four sisters and they all sought to have a share in him. He was not allowed to play outside his own garden but he did not find his own company inadequate for he was a versatile little boy and had many interests.

His parents prided themselves on freedom of thought and he was initiated into the activities of the birds and the bees at

169

a tender age. His father studied books on the subject and fed his son's inquiring mind on carefully chosen extracts.

Jeremy's maternal grandmother was a patient of mine. She was a widow and three of her four daughters had escaped her via marriage but Mary, the youngest, dutifully stayed home. She was good-natured and gentle and thirty-one; if she mourned her wasted youth it was only to herself. Momma had once kept a market stall and done very well out of it, but her daughters preferred to forget their humble beginnings. Even Jeremy grieved that she was so cultureless. Once after a day in the country he explained to her the function of the catkin and how it was that the hazel tree came to have a little nut, but she cackled bawdily, 'S'truth! 'E'll be a don 'ond when it cums ter puttin' a bun in th'oven!'

Jeremy was perplexed; cooking was not his métier.

One evening a week the two elder sisters took over to give Mary a night out. She usually reciprocated by sitting in for Jeremy's parents until it happened that art classes were started at the local night school and then, to everyone's surprise, she decided to enrol.

Momma took refuge in ridicule. 'At your age! They'll bost o' loffin!'

On the first evening Mary got cold feet and nearly funked it; only Momma's mockery spurred her on. Her fellow students were a cosmopolitan lot; two arty youths in matching sweaters and trews held hands caressingly; both flaunted shoulder-length hair and chained medallions. Embarrassed she looked away, but they were later revealed as a husband and wife employing togetherness. There was a coloured bus driver still in uniform, a nun, a group of lively teenagers and two housewives, matronly and reassuring.

Mary stood hesitantly at the art teacher's desk as he bent over the register and he looked up inquiringly. In that moment their two lives fell into one predestined pattern. After class he escorted her home and by the time they got there they knew all that was important about each other. William was thirty-six and unattached; neither of them had time to waste. Marriage was a foregone conclusion and as they parted on the porch in the gathering dusk the bobowlers blundered into them unnoticed.

Until Mary got into the house she had completely forgotten Momma, but her state of grace betrayed her for Momma was immediately susceptible to anything which might affect herself and Mary was too naive to resort to subterfuge. Cocooned in wonder she was impervious to derision and disbelief. Momma withdrew her taunts, frustrated and frenzied.

For days the family remained stunned. Momma was the first to recover and shrewdly reviewed the situation. She had now met William and recognized in him a supervisory force. Not up her street by a long chalk! She couldn't abide bossy blokes!

With a Blackcountry woman's talent for converting unavoidable misfortune into something advantageous she began plotting her future. After much cogitation she reckoned that if she let William and Mary rent her house and honoured each of her daughters with her presence for three months a year she would both supplement her income and also have a finger in everyone's pie, a joy she had long yearned for.

While the family were still stupefied she called a conclave and informed them of her plans. They were dumbstruck at this fresh disaster. Jeremy alone rejoiced; his new uncle had embellished his scrapbook with fine illustrations of his botanical specimens and had promised that he should participate in the nuptials as a page boy. His cup was brimming over.

The great day dawned and the respective families, resplendent in festive attire, flanked the aisle. Momma, crammed into new corsets, longed for release. Through the stained glass windows the sun blessed William and Mary with a rosy glow; behind them stood Jeremy, sailor-suited and anticipatory. This was the first *homo sapiens* union of his experience and he was breathless with excitement. It was a moving ceremony and when it was over a momentary silence filled the little church. Jeremy could contain himself no longer; into the hushed solemnity rose his clear treble.

'Uncle. Are you going to give Auntie your pollen now or when we get home?'

*　　*　　*

I was surprised to find that one of my diabetic patients was a spiritualist – she looked so normal – but once when Judith, then a small child, was with me she showed great interest in her and had an aura of suppressed excitement. The next day, when I was alone, she asked me to bring Judith again for she had seen, on the back of her head, the sign of a cross and wished to investigate it.

I opted out as graciously as possible for I knew her to be a very sincere person and shortly afterwards she moved to another area to care for her sister who was ill – and then died herself!

Now you'd have thought she'd have had an inkling of that wouldn't you?

When Judith was nine years old she injured her ankle and had to rest it for several weeks. During her enforced inactivity she wrote numerous letters and recorded many songs on grandad's tape-recorder. She had a high sweet voice, rather like Grandma Leeds, and she sang old-fashioned ditties taught to her by Mother, quaint little songs from a bygone era imparting knowledge of the social graces.

> When they're laughing with you –
> When they like you so –
> When they want to keep you –
> That's the time to go.

One day when I returned home my neighbour was waiting for me with an anxious expression and a telegram – but it was addressed to Judith, surely a mistake? I agreed, but post is sacrosanct so we let Judith open it. It read:

'We're afraid you're a little too young to be our Cotton Queen but a special prize of five guineas is on its way to you with our love. See this week's paper. Editor *Women's Sunday Mirror*.'

172

When questioned she admitted to having entered the *Mirror*'s competition to find a Cotton Queen, filling in the questionaire. She had measured herself with my tape measure, and submitted a full-length photograph. She had plenty of those taken in dancing costumes.

We waited anxiously for the next edition. Judith's photograph was prominently displayed, together with the headlines 'She is 22 – 22 – 22 and wants to be our Cotton Queen!'

*   *   *

My breakfast was geared to time – Bemax laced with milk and sugar, nutrious, speedy, but hardly filling. By midday I had an aching void crying out to be filled, but if I came home for a meal invariably I found someone laying in wait for me so that I was diverted from my planned routine and lost my dinner anyway.

One day, seduced by a wonderful whiff of fish 'n' chips, I followed my nose and found the shop still open. It was empty of customers but an overweight assistant perched on a high stool was killing time by picking her nose, rolling the results into little pellets and flicking them across the counter. My hunger fled and so did I.

When eventually I reached home it was to find a young fellow anxiously waiting for me. His mother had suffered a stroke and he bore a doctor's note requesting that I should attend immediately. I paused long enough to put the dinner on a low heat so that it would be partly cooked when GL got home, then I went, taking the young man with me.

His mother had indeed had a stroke – but five days previously, since when she had been lying unattended on a bed of excreta. The rest of her family, congregated gloomily in the kitchen, hadn't thought to do anything about it.

When I took a bowl of warm water upstairs and rolled the old lady on her side the stench of ammonia so stung my eyes and nostrils that at first I didn't see the hundreds of pound notes, grossly fouled, on which she had been lying. Obviously her life savings on which she had lain every night for security. I scooped them up, sodden and filthy as they were, dumped them in the bowl and advised the stunned family to cleanse and cool-iron them before taking them to a bank; they might as well be doing something.

By the time I had got the patient clean and wholesome it was very late and when I got back the family had already dined. But the first thing I noticed was an ominous message on the telephone pad marked 'Very urgent'.

'I've had enough!' I exploded. 'Nobody should have to live like this! Tomorrow I shall give in my notice. We can manage all right if we give up the car.'

The girls stared wide-eyed and open-mouthed; my husband remained silent. His silence always spoke louder than words but this time I meant it and I flounced out full of righteous indignation.

I still had the late night morphias to visit but I went to the new case first. The morphia patients would bear with me knowing that never would they, of all people, be omitted.

My new victim was a fine brawny fellow suffering surprisingly from impacted faeces. He was getting a lot of abdominal pain and hospitalization depended on my results. Fear leaked out of his eyes for he dreaded an operation and was convinced he had cancer from which his wife had died several years previously. He had not passed flatus for a very long time and that I assured him could be the cause of all his pain.

When I inserted a gloved and lubricated finger into his rectum I met with a hard unyielding mass of faeces; after much probing I was able to dislodge a little but discouragingly an enema was returned clear. Turning him on his left side I then ran in a small amount of warm glycerine and sat beside him on the bed pressing his buttocks together in an effort to get him to retain it. While waiting for it to take effect we discussed the problem which had brought him to this pass.

As a man living alone his diet had been the most simple: an egg for breakfast, canteen fried dinner with chips and suet pudding, and bread and cheese for supper. He had given up his customary pint at the pub under the illusion that anything you enjoy must be bad for you. That I told him was a great mistake. His nightly tipple would do him more good than anything; bran with his breakfast was also to be recommended, with fresh vegetables at dinnertime and maybe a few pitted prunes, instead of that stodgey pud. The bowel habit varies from person to person and it is quite normal for some people to perform only on alternate days. Constipation is present when the stools are hard and dry, and it is important therefore that the fluid intake is adequate.

When I had entertained my captive victim to this absorbing lecture in order to take his mind off the effects of the glycerine, he told me that his doctor had been pre-scribing 'Dulcolax' suppositories for a long time but they had been quite ineffective. I pricked up my ears at this – I've known folk take them by mouth before now. But no, this chap had more sense than that. He'd followed the directions on the box implicitly.

After about twenty minutes I gave him an enema saponis and then supported him on a bucket. In the loo it is impossible to examine the result. There was an explosive and very rewarding outcome and when he had finished I helped him back to bed for by then the poor fellow was quite exhausted. After investigating the issue I took it over to show him; people get great satisfaction in seeing for themselves what they have actually done.

There was a mass of constipated faeces and a great deal of silver paper. He had followed the instructions about lubricating and inserting the suppositories – it was a shame they hadn't told him to remove the silver wrapping first.

We parted amicably. He was a changed man, buoyant with relief, and I got great satisfaction out of rousing the doctor from his bed to tell him hospitalization wasn't necessary after all. There is nothing more rewarding than a job successfully accomplished and I went lightheartedly to my belated morphias, who prefer to be done as late as possible since it ensures a better night.

175

When I got home the street was dark and silent and the only light showing was ours, a subdued one on the landing. The family was abed. I had a quick snack and a stand-up bath in the kitchen, anxious not to disturb them. My husband was fast asleep. I crept into bed and lay on the extreme edge fearing to wake him – I could do without that tonight.

There was a soft pattering of feet and Judith stood at the bedside; in the half-light her face was puckered and distressed.

'Mom, you didn't mean what you said did you – about giving up your job?'

'Why, dear, you'd like me to be home, wouldn't you? To have more time for you?'

'Yes, Mom but – ' She twisted the hem of her nightie around a forefinger in an effort to explain her dilemma.

'You see, Mom, it's like this: I'm the only girl at our school whose mother is a district nurse.'

CHAPTER TEN

— Out and About —

IT WAS WITH mixed feelings that I heard that Torti Collis was planning to pay us a brief visit. Anything that made extra work was unwelcome, but it was only to break her journey between Canterbury, where she worked, and the Lake District where she was holidaying with a friend.

We had kept in touch in a desultory sort of way and it would be grand to see her again, but not on my home ground where her sharp eyes and caustic wit would observe and record my lack of domesticity.

It was as though scales had fallen from my eyes. The curtains were dingy, the kitchen needed decorating and there was verdigris on the brasses. I hastened to amend what I could but it was certainly too late for the kitchen.

She drove a little MG and her clothes were very smart if rather risqué. She had plumped up a bit and it suited her. I saw GL eyeing her décolleté neck-line and hurried her to her room to unpack. She couldn't find her curlers so I gave her a bagful out of a drawer and told her magnanimously she could keep them.

The evening meal went well: the beef was delicious, the Yorkshire pudding was as light as a feather and Elizabeth's lemon meringue pie was *par excellence*. Gun-layer was on night duty and having bribed the girls to bed with the television we settled down to a good cant. Torti was now an industrial nurse; if there was an accident she sent for an ambulance, otherwise she just doled out STs and aspirin and stuck on the occasional plaster.

177

'I never lift anything heavier than a cup of tea,' she boasted and I groaned – trust Torti to come up smelling of roses! After a bath she sat by the fire in her dressing gown and began putting in her curlers. When I saw them I gasped in horror. However could I have given her those – they were riffy!

'I'm so sorry, Torti. I'd no idea those curlers were so dirty!' I couldn't abase myself enough – 'Why they're absolutely FILTHY!'

Torti eyed me coldly. 'These,' she said 'are mine. I did find them after all.'

* * *

This was my weekend on duty alone; nearly thirty routine visits for Sunday had already been increased by a trickle of new cases. I set off at seven-thirty. Two enemas awaited me, both urgent since hospitalization depended on the results. Inevitably they were very time consuming and I had a slow puncture, which meant I had to use my foot pump to keep going. Eventually I returned home for GL to change the tyre; any hurt to the car he took as a personal affront and he did a lot of tutting over the ill treatment it had suffered. Five new cases for penicillin awaited my attention and from then on it became obvious that flu was rampant amongst the immigrants. I groaned. Oh the language problem! Communication must be established by mime (imagine trying to find out whether or not a coloured patient has had his bowels moved!).

The first three victims lived in the same tenement building. There was no response from the front door so I tried the back. After a great commotion of bolts and keys the door was finally opened on a chain. I was inspected, drawn inside, the hardware replaced, and the keeper of the door dropped the key into his pocket and indicated the stairs. The building was three storeys high; each floor was covered with pallet beds on which men were recumbent and as many men again littered the stairs. Sunday was a bad day, for during the week half of them worked on the day-shift and half on nights, so that the pallets were constantly occupied; today there was a double complement and they were hard put to find parking space.

My patients, also on pallet beds and on the third floor, looked very ill indeed. I spoke to them gently; they couldn't understand what I was saying but I hoped that the tone of my voice would reassure them. Dark eyes followed my every movement with apprehension as I prepared the injections. Since it had been established that some people have an intolerance of penicillin a trial dose is first given, the remainder being given later if no ill-effects are apparent. In each case the initial dose was borne stoically, but when I approached with the second they reacted violently, wagging forefingers before my face to indicate one and only one was prescribed! The second injection was imperative so I carried on regardless, and they lay back on their pallets resigned to a quick demise from what they were convinced was an overdose. Now that non-allergy had been established only one jab daily would be necessary for the rest of the course and so I would be condemned as a novice out to practise on them.

When I descended the stairs a deputation awaited me. I was ushered into the kitchen and seated on the only chair. Obviously they had been told that to offer a cup of tea was the done thing, and they were not to know I never imbibed tea on my round; what they did know was that protocol was of paramount importance and they were determined to observe it. With horror I watched as the tea, sugar, milk and water were all tipped into the kettle and boiled together. Only when I had consumed a mug of the scalding and revolting brew did the doorkeeper produce his key and let me out.

Inevitably many more fell foul of the bug but they all recovered. During the ensuing weeks I formed a good rapport with them but they always wore their turbans, I never saw another woman in the house, and their behaviour was exemplary.

The next two patients were more difficult to find as I'd

been given the wrong address. Conditions were much the same and their reactions to the second jab even more protesting. I came away feeling depressed and professionally inadequate. Outside I found GL seeking me; three more immigrants had been phoned in and he wished to save me the journey home.

My new patients lived in an area where the houses were old but had class. The one I was looking for was immediately obvious since it flaunted a frontage of violet and pea green, a screaming comparison with the sombre black and white of its neighbours. In each room, visible through the open doorways, men could be seen demonstrating their culinary arts over gas-rings, frying pans were flourished and an odour of curry and spice pervaded the air. On seeing me several came out and smilingly gesticulated towards a closed door. I knocked and was admitted to a room where three people were clustered round a paraffin heater. There was a very handsome woman, a man and a most beautiful child of about seven years. The child had the face of a cherub; her huge dark eyes were fringed with long sweeping lashes and her black springy curls fell to below the waist.

None of the occupants looked ill but they produced vials of penicillin to substantiate their claim. I prepared the injection and the man obligingly proffered himself but the woman intervened and loosening her clothing arranged herself gracefully on the bed. She accepted both injections with the satisfaction of one who felt she was getting her money's worth. Mollified I admired the child who seemed to comprehend a little; children are usually the first to learn a new language. Patting her curls I congratulated them on having so lovely a daughter. She was, I said, the most beautiful little girl I had ever seen. The parents, sensing a compliment, smiled and nodded graciously; the angel child made a very rude gesture. Rebuffed I went in search of the next patient.

He lay on a bed which shook beneath him, whether with fear or a rigor was not at first apparent. I made soothing noises and turned away to make my preparations. When I

180

returned to the bed it was empty, as was the room. I peered under the bed and from its sanctuary saucer eyes peered back at me. I squatted on the floor and made more soothing noises, but he retreated out of reach and as I moved to the other side of the bed he shuffled back. I could dismiss him as having refused treatment but that was to admit defeat; he obviously needed antibiotics and without them would almost certainly develop pneumonia. Despoiling my white apron I shuffled bellywise after him and grabbed an ankle; his other foot jerked out catching me on the nose and blood gushed forth over both of us.

Eventually shuffling back from under the bed I dragged him protesting loudly in my wake. As we emerged he arched his back, giving it a violent clout against the iron framework of the bed, and bellowed with pain. Quickly I was astride him and exposing the afflicted area. There appeared to be no damage but I applied gentle massage. I'm told that I have a soothing touch and gradually he relaxed and lay prone under my kneading fingers. My nose had ceased to bleed and mentally I gauged the upper and outer quadrant of his buttock, the site of the injection. The prepared syringe in a disposable towel lay on the bed within reach. Quick as a flash I reached for it and plunged the needle home! This time he got the lot; no second jab for him. A round of applause came from the doorway where an audience had gathered unseen. Bloody but unbowed I helped him back to bed. I had adrenalin at the ready in case of a reaction but he suffered no ill-effects. I appeared to have come off worst and my conscience smote me, for never had I given so unsterile an injection.

Making exaggerated motions of ablution I confronted the little crowd in the doorway. One obligingly brought me a bowl of water with which I cleansed first my patient then myself, taking off my apron and using the less gory parts as a towel. The sight of so much blood had sobered them all; there was no way of explaining to them that it was mine!

On the next floor the last patient lay quietly in his bed; dark eyes surveyed me from a brown face. This time I would stand no nonsense. I smiled silently and went over to the window to prepare the dose. Looking down into the yard below I saw the angel child urinating against a wall – at least that explained the rude gesture! I returned to the bed determined to preserve my professional dignity and addressed the patient in a loud clear voice.

'Doctor,' I assumed the familiar stance adopted by his general practitioner, 'want me,' beating my chest, 'give you,' touching his, 'needle!' With a flourish I produced the syringe.

Incredulity passed over his face as he raised himself on one elbow. 'Why,' he said in astonishment, 'can't you speak English?'

* * *

Mrs Tibbs put on both pairs of specs, one behind the other, and settled down to read the previous evening's local paper which I had just left with her. She didn't mind her news secondhand since it was for free, and on alternate Fridays Mrs Buggins took the accumulated papers to the fish and chip shop and exchanged them for chips which, doused with vinegar, they found very tasty.

Her main interest lay in the births, marriages and deaths, 'hatches, matches and dispatches', and by keeping a record of the matches on her calendar she was able at a later date to team them up with the hatches and get some very interesting results. Wedlock she reckoned was nothing more than four legs in a bed, adding pithily, 'The fust three months yo' could ate it an' the next three months yo' wish yo' 'ad!'

Buggins, she reflected, was a long time coming but Mrs Buggins had other fish to fry. Doll, her daughter, whose status had improved since her marriage, had kept her at arm's length for years but now she sought a reconciliation. After all you only had one mother; also she had three children and could do with a baby sitter. When she was asked to sit in Mrs Buggins was flattered and very willing. She donned her best clobber, the red plush hat, twopence from a jumble sale, the black, out-dated astrakhan coat

182

from the same source and of course the men's boots which were so accommodating to her bunions.

'Wheer bin yo' gooin'?' demanded Mrs Tibbs suspiciously when she finally put in an appearance.

'I'm gooin' to our Doll's to mind the kids,' announced Mrs Buggins, 'while 'er an' Perce goo's to the pitchers.'

'I should think yo' bin!' cried Mrs Tibbs. 'Yer saft sod yo'!'

'I bin as I bin!' retorted Mrs Buggins defiantly, making her exit with all the dignity she could muster.

'Red 'at an' no breeches!' Mrs Tibbs hurled the final insult. 'Goo an' joy goo with yer!'

When Mrs Buggins presented herself on her daughter's threshold, Doll dragged her hastily inside before the neighbours caught sight of her. Those boots! And that hat! Quickly she divested her mother of her outer garments. Mrs Buggins wore a clean pinny over her other clothes. 'Take it off,' begged Doll. 'You haven't come to work!' But when she had stripped her mother of the offending garment and revealed what was underneath she hurridly tied it on again. 'Never mind,' she compromised. 'You can do the washing up.'

Already she regretted the reunion. Percival had been very much against it and she was now anxious to get him out of the house before he made contact with his mother-in-law. The twins, Mandy and Marilyn, and their little brother Errol, already pyjama'd and supped, were watching television; they could stay up until the end of their programme, said Doll, and she admonished them to behave for Grandma. She left a snack in the kitchen in case her Mother got peckish, and was gone.

No sooner had their parents departed than Marilyn began twiddling the television knobs.

'Er! Yo' moent do that!' cried Mrs Buggins anxiously.

'It' our telly isn't it?' snapped Mandy, quick to defend her twin.

'Why yo' cheeky little sod!' screeched Mrs Buggins, beginning to wish she hadn't come.

183

Marilyn sniffed and remarked loftily, 'Somebody has "let off".' All three children stared pointedly at their grand-mother who made a confused exit.

In the kitchen she found a hunk of pork pie, an apple tart and a bottle of stout. She would enjoy them better at home so she wrapped them up and transferred them to her bag. No good letting them go to waste. Next she went in search of the WC. It was a toilet-cum-bathroom and she was very impressed; the bath and the 'bog' were in matching pink, as were the bath mat and the mat surrounding the pedestal, beside which was a container with a pink plastic lavatory brush. Doll, she remembered, had always favoured pink. The colour scheme was relieved by blue plastic curtains and a row of birds in full flight affixed to the far wall. Even the Queen, decided Mrs Buggins, could not have bettered this.

Later she made a tour of the bedrooms and enjoyed having a good mooch. Doll, she decided with satisfaction, had done well for herself. The connubial bed in particular attracted her: it looked so very comfortable and irresistibly inviting to her poor old feet. She loosened her boots and lay down on it, pulling the pink satin quilt over herself. In no time at all she was asleep.

When Doll and Percival returned they were scandalized to find the children watching the late night movie. 'But we're granny sitting,' they cried defensively and guttural snores from above substantiated their claim.

Mrs Buggins trudged home in high dudgeon. What a shindy they had kicked up just because she was having a little kip on their bed. Snotty-nosed buggers! She must never let Mrs Tibbs know how right she had been. She decided to ignore their recent fracas and offer the stout as a peace offering.

Mrs Tibbs was still up and accepted the stout graciously, reciprocating by taking out two mugs and pouring half in each. In return Mrs Buggins produced the pie and apple tart and the two old ladies settled down to a midnight repast. When repleted Mrs Tibbs brushed away the crumbs. 'Well?' she queried, indicating that a state of confidence had been reached, and Mrs Buggins needed no second bidding. Mrs Tibbs listened, deducting all she heard by half to allow for exaggerations and Mrs Buggins, knowing she would do this, overstated accordingly. Doll's home took on new dimensions: the rooms became carpeted, the curtains luxuriant, the closet alone needed no codding but she enthused on the 'flight of swallers', the pretty mats and the pink lavatory brush.

'Though mind yer, Tibbs,' she reflected thoughtfully, returning to more mundane matters, 'I'd sooner 'ave a bit of paper meself. S'truth, them brushes doh 'arf scratch yer arse!'

*   *   *

It was a real pea-souper, rimed with frost, the night Mrs Buggins roused me to say that Mrs Tibbs was blowing her whistle.

There had been several tragedies when old people had fallen and died of exposure because they were unable to attract attention to their plight. Many suggestions had been put forward to safeguard against this and one was that aged persons, living alone, should be given a card, 'Nurse required', to put in the window in the event of such an emergency. The cards were issued but rarely used since most victims were unable to reach either the card or the window when the occasion arose.

Alarm bells were the next device to be considered but these proved to be just as inaccessible as the cards to anyone floored and on their back. I had the temerity to suggest police whistles and approached the authorities both verbally and in writing but was told they were unsuitable as they would only bring the police running (and what would be wrong with that?). However I went my own way, publicizing my idea and kitting out my most vulnerable patients with a lanyard round the neck to which a whistle was attached and so knotted that they could not choke themselves and it was always on their person. I explained to neighbours so that whistle blowing would be investigated

185

and this was the first time that Mrs Tibbs had need of it.

I had to break a small pane to unlatch the kitchen window and climb in. Mrs Tibbs lay on her back like a beetle and just as helpless. Her left hand was twisted under her at an abnormal angle, surely fractured, but otherwise she appeared to be suffering only from shock and cold. We managed to hoist her into bed and between blankets; the fire was out but the bricks she always kept in the oven instead of hot water bottles were still very warm and we wrapped them in their flannel bags and put them in with her. I bound up her injured wrist, at which juncture she began to cuss heartily and we knew then she would be all right. We all had piping hot cocoa and Mrs Buggins obligingly offered to sleep with her to keep her warm.

The next morning Mrs Tibbs was up as usual, established in her big chair. She had removed the trappings from her wrist but it was obviously still painful. Both of her hands and wrists were so swollen and distorted with arthritis that it was difficult to ascertain the damage and I went away to phone her doctor. He was just off to an urgent call but promised to see her later; meanwhile he arranged an ambulance to take her for X-ray.

When I returned to Mrs Tibbs and told her she bucked like a startled horse. She had never been in hospital but she was convinced that they were inhabited by fanatical surgeons lurking to experiment on the unwary.

'If they get me under gas,' she haggled, 'then it's God knows what the varmints'll be up to!' Compresses of comfry, she insisted, would soon put it right. At this point the ambulance men arrived and it took our combined efforts to wheedle her into the vehicle, though she recovered sufficiently to hurl abuse at the small group of onlookers and shook her good fist at me as a parting shot.

She was on my mind all morning for I was really very concerned about her. She was now in her late eighties and no match for the modern medico. As soon as I could find the time I returned, but she was already home looking very smug and Mrs Buggins was out in the garden gathering comfry. The offending wrist was not encased in plaster as I had expected it to be and there was a note confirming that there was nothing wrong except chronic arthritis. I felt very guilty, making all that fuss for nothing. Poor old girl, it had been such a needless ordeal for her. 'I am sorry,' I said apologetically. 'You know I really did think they would find that you had a fracture there.'

'I dey,' grinned Mrs Tibbs toothlessly. 'I give 'em the wrong 'ond!'

*　　*　　*

Elizabeth looked at me speculatively. 'You know,' she said, 'I think an eyeliner might help you, Mom.'

I was rather taken aback for I hadn't realized I needed help, but mostly I was gratified to find that someone still took an interest in my appearance. So the next time I went to the chemists, at the end of my miscellaneous list I added eyeliner.

The man looked perplexed by my unusual request, for my purchases are normally limited to catheters, lubricants and glycerine suppositories.

'Eyeliner, nurse?' he queried, scratching the back of his head (I have quite a rapport with chemists and undertakers which I realize is stimulated by my profession rather than my own peculiar type of charm). 'Eyeliner now, not much in my line.' He laughed nervously at his own little pun. 'Perhaps we should get one of the girls.'

'Oh no!' I protested. Dolly birds diminish me. 'I'll find it myself.'

I rummaged among the alien goods on his counter until I found eyeliners; apparently there was a choice of either a pencil or a small bottle of dark liquid to which a fine camel-hair brush was attached. I settled for the liquid – painting is my hobby – and I had taken a fancy to the camel-hair brush.

I made a quick escape, thankful that my purchase had not been observed by some joker; my friend the chemist still looked anxious. I couldn't wait to try out my new beauty aid and as soon as I reached home I closeted myself in the bathroom and, still hampered by my hat, endeavoured to follow the directions.

'With the brush paint a line as near as possible to the lashes,' they instructed. This called for time and concentration – and a very steady hand – but before long someone was clamouring to get in and hurriedly I washed it off.

The following morning with quite a youthful stirring in my blood I rose at five-thirty and, when my usual chores were done, settled down in the fierce light of the kitchen to do justice to my face. With advancing age and close contact with streptomycin my eyelids had tended to thicken and wrinkle, not at all conducive to painting on, but I persevered and thought the result quite pleasing, albeit a little bog-eyed. I could hardly wait to try myself out and escaped before the family had recovered from the trauma of getting up.

The diabetics were my first concern; until I had got them out of my hair I didn't consider my day had begun. The first patient was of such long-standing she qualified as an old friend. Half-closing her eyes she regarded me with compassion: 'Yo've bin called out in the night agin. I con see it in thee eyes, yo' look 'arf jed!'

I didn't dally any longer than was necessary.

The second patient didn't comment. He was very short-sighted but he asked if I would take his prescription to the chemist whose shop lay en route to the next patient.

My friend the pharmacist was openly amused. While he dealt with the prescription the entire staff emerged each in turn from their inner sanctum, obviously to view me; he *must* have told them. I detected giggling amongst the dolly birds.

Shouting that I would return later for the prescription I made a confused exit. The chemist was no longer my friend; worse still, he was disloyal. In future I would take my custom elsewhere and with it all those lucrative prescriptions the patients asked me to collect. Comforted by thoughts of revenge but with my ego deflated I stumbled into the kitchen of patient number three.

She took one look and embraced me.

'Doh tell me!' she cried. 'I con see, yo've got one of yer 'eads agin. 'Ow about a cupper char? Or' (in a conspiratorial whisper, though no one else was in earshot), ''ow about a wet?' As a female body living alone she was earmarked by us all as a convenient pennyhouse and she gloried in being the chosen.

'No thank you, dear,' I said as I disengaged myself and made for the sink. 'But there's some mud in my eye. Could I possible have a little swill?'

The camel-hair brush is very useful.

* * *

When Elizabeth was seventeen she was accepted at the local hospital with a view to training as a nurse. On her birthday card I wrote:

Well dear, another year has passed –
I don't know why they go so fast,
They never went with such a wrench
When you were just a little wench,
But now alas they leap apace
And linger only on my face.
A lifetime is a fleeting thing
But always sweeter in the spring
For all the world is fresh and green
When you are only seventeen.

Judith was delighted with it. 'Promise, Mom, promise you'll write one for me when I'm seventeen. Cross your heart and spit over your little finger.' I crossed my heart and spat. She was addicted to doggerel and on the last Parents' Day at her school one of her own composition had embellished the classroom wall:

My mother is a district nurse,
But often patients just get worse,
Then when she has gone to bed

189

Someone comes to say they're dead
And though it makes my Father shout
She has to go and lay them out.

Judith had been to dancing school from an early age and dancing had now become a very important part of her life. She had a string of medals, silver and gold, hanging like horse brasses on one of Bo'sun's old collars. Every autumn some of the older girls auditioned for the Christmas pantomime at Dudley Hippodrome, but they had to be twelve years old to qualify. I thought they looked weary after the first two months and was reluctant to let Judith participate, but she pleaded so that it was difficult to refuse.

Madame's dancing school had a high reputation and there was a great demand for her pupils. Judith was auditioned and accepted, and a licence obtained from the educational authorities granting her leave from school. Rules were strict; the junior troupe were closely chaperoned and attended classes daily with a qualified teacher, though priority was given to practising their parts in the panto.

Robinson Crusoe was the theme and several well-known personalities from television took the principal parts. The excitement was life blood to Judith and I thought ruefully that she would never have forgiven us had we not let her take part.

Elizabeth had been delighted to get away from home but still came back every day in her off-duty to agonize over her patients and the persecution of predatory ward sisters. I could see that she would be easy prey, for even as a child she would never defend herself with a fib whatever the circumstances.

One of Elizabeth's duties apparently was to push the dressing trolly for the staff nurse – only she pushed it into the large aquarium in the middle of the ward, smashing it, flooding the ward and doing the fish no good. She wept over them and the L plates they put on her trolly.

One day she came home with a besotted expression. 'Oh Mom, I've met a wonderful boy!' She'd had several boy-

190

friends but Ivan was the last. He was a very energetic young man with a determined chin and a trench coat; I'd always been partial to trench coats. He also had a most pleasing speaking voice, and that was something else I was partial to. In no time the young couple were engaged and planning to marry when Elizabeth had finished her training.

At last after weeks of rehearsal the pantomime opened on Boxing Day and it went without a hitch. It was my day off as I had worked Christmas Day, and Father treated us all to the show. Judith had been pantomiming for the past six years but now that she was twelve it was her first time as a professional. Expectantly we sat perched on the red plush tip up seats and Mother's joy was complete.

During the next two weeks flu decimated the cast but Judith escaped it and never once missed a show. When one of the acrobatic troupe had to opt out permanently she was asked to fill the gap, but the costumes needed speedy alterations and I spent one frantic night covering a helmet and leotard with emerald green sequins. I was quite boss-eyed the next day. Every morning she went in by bus but at night after the last performance she had to be met and escorted home. This was her father's job except when he was on the night-shift. We were the ones who wilted, Judy was inexhaustable. In the past few weeks she had matured, suddenly becoming instant girl, vivid and scintillating.

Meanwhile the weather was deteriorating and the flu spreading. Several of my colleagues succumbed to it and the working day became inevitably longer. One ominously dark afternoon as I came through Owen Street a shop window made gold with daffodils halted me and I bought two bunches for Mother. When I called she and Dad were sitting in the half-light watching Eileen Fowler's keep fit class on the television. As she espied me Mother cried, 'You'll surely catch your death, going around half naked. Why ever don't you wear a scarf?'

'Now then, you sitting there in your armchair,' called Eileen straight out of the box. 'You wouldn't need to muffle up to keep warm if you did your exercises.'

'Why daze my 'ide!' exclaimed Mother agast. 'I do believe she means me.' Nothing would convince her otherwise, so I laid the flowers in her lap. 'Here's your first bit of spring, Mom.'

As I bent to kiss her goodbye she tugged at the lapels of my coat and with a wary eye on the television whispered defiantly, 'Do fastern your neck up.'

The wind which had abated a little sprang up in the evening with renewed fury, lashing with frozen snow all who were so injudicious as to venture forth. Elizabeth and GL were both on night-duty and Judith was still tripping the light fantastic.

That night when I went to collect her a storm raged and maniacal gusts of wind battered the car as we slithered home past the hospital with a thought for Elizabeth doing her stint in the darkened wards. The snow had drifted now, obliterating familiar landmarks and giving an eerie beauty to what had been a stark industrial landscape. We were like strangers in a far country.

At last we reached home. Thankfully I bedded the car and went indoors. Judith already had the kettle on and was making bacon sandwiches. She had a prodigious appetite and we munched them over a glowing fire, heartened to have escaped the elements. Judy stretched languorously like a kitten.

'Saturday tomorrow, an extra performance,' she said with satisfaction, but I had begun to doze and getting no response she prodded me mischievously.

'Come on you old sluggaluck. Up the wooden hill!'

I mumbled vexatiously, thinking she'd got a streak of Mother in her too as ruthlessly she propelled me up the stairs before her.

The voice of the wind had changed to a perfidious soughing, making a mockery of our complacency, sated with the toll which, despite everything, it had already taken from us.

I woke in the early hours of the following morning with the lingering flavour of disturbing dreams. Somewhere in

192

the darkness a sad spirit keened its loss and I felt around for familiar things with which to reassure myself. It was some time before I realized that the keening was not an extension of my dream, and it was accompanied by a rattling of the letterbox. Unshod I sped down the stairs and switched on the hall light. The flap of the letterbox opened and through the aperture floated Father's disembodied voice, 'Edie, Edie, I think your Mother's dead!'

I threw open the door and sought to draw him inside but he evaded me, fey and distraught, snow frosting his white poll.

'Come in, Dad, while I get the car out.'

'No, I must go to her, perhaps – ' Beseechingly his eyes begged for hope, then he escaped me into the darkness, his stumbling footsteps crunching on the frozen snow.

With numbed fingers I dressed and got the car out hoping to overtake him, but snow blocked the driveway and the roads, treacherous and untraversed, demanded caution. When I arrived the doors were open wide and Father sat, head in hands, crouched over the dead ashes in the fireplace. The usually snug room was cold and comfortless and a chill breeze from the open door fluttered the serenity of the daffodils.

I hurried upstairs.

It wasn't Mother, warm and whimsical, but a stranger fashioned from cold clay, and the familiar sweet sickly scent of death pervaded the air. I fell on my knees at the bedside clutching her worn, unresponsive hand.

'Oh no, Mother, not you! Not you!' But it was myself I was sobbing for and for my grievous loss.

After a while I rose and straightened her limbs, removing the blankets and covering her with a sheet. Before going downstairs I took a towel from the washstand and scoured my ravaged face. Father, still crouching in her chair, looked up, his eyes pleading for a miracle, but sadly I shook my head. With a despairing gesture he went over to the window and closed the curtains, shutting out the dawn.

I took his hand, which was nearly as cold as Mother's.

'It's the way she would have wanted to go, quietly, in her own bed, with you beside her.' But he refused comfort.

'Why did she go without me? How could she leave me?' he lamented. 'Last night I didn't say my prayers, it was so cold. This is my punishment.' He confessed it like a child stricken with guilt.

'I didn't notice anything wrong – I ought to have known.'

'No, she was herself, enjoyed her food and watched the telly. Then last night Sally came crying, said her husband was going to die. Your Mom would go to see if she could do anything for him.'

I saw her, a woman past eighty, struggling over the steep treacherous slope of Watery Lane Crossing in a winter blizzard to comfort a man who would probably recover in a few days, as indeed he did.

After she returned, cold, fatigued and buffeted by the wind, they went to bed and during the night Father had roused to find her awake too.

'Father, I do feel bad.'

Alarmed he switched on the light, but she looked beautiful with a lovely rosy glow.

'Shall I get Edie?'

'No, no! Wait until morning.'

Sleep was sacred. Never would she disturb anyone if she could help. After a while he put off the light and they lay holding hands in the darkness until he slept again. When he woke at five o'clock her hand, still within his, was inert and cold.

For want of something to do I brewed tea for both of us. Automatically Father took from the cupboard his large white beaker and Mother's cup, delicately flowered and paper thin, her one extravagance – dainty china. Still forgetful he sugared them both liberally and when I drank the scalding sweet beverage the unaccustomed sugar put new life into me.

'I can't do anything else until the doctor is notified because it's so long since he saw her. You know that complicates things, don't you?' He nodded.

'When he's been shall I get that woman from down the road to lay her out? It doesn't seem right for you – '

'No!' I said fiercely. 'No one else must touch her.' But as I said it I knew that she must also be handled by strangers with harsh probing hands and I thanked God that Father knew nothing of post-mortems.

'I must go now, Dad.' I kissed him. 'Harry will come and stay with you until I get back.'

'You'll let Hilda know?'

'Of course, dear.' He put out a hand to detain me.

'Don't tell Judy, not until tonight, then she'll have Sunday to get over the shock. She has a big day today and Grandma wouldn't want her to miss a show. She was so proud of her.'

Outside the daylight dazzled me and the garden was a white wonderland. Under their blanket of snow her lupins, lilies and grape hyacinths slept. Never again would she gather roses, pick damsons for her jam and sit in the shade of the apple trees charming us with her nonsense.

I found Judith still abed. Elizabeth and Gun-layer were stunned and shaken. Together we composed a telegram. Poor Hilda! What a blow I must deal her. Should I say Mother was ill to break it more gently? 'No.' said my husband; it must be swift and final and addressed to John.

'Regret Mother died peacefully in her sleep.'

The sending of it put the final stamp on her demise.

195

CHAPTER ELEVEN

— Judith —

U<small>NTIL</small> M<small>OTHER</small> <small>DIED</small> we never realized how loved and respected she was in the neighbourhood, but in retrospect there was never anything derogatory that could have been said of her.

All along the route of her funeral cortège people stood silently. I would hitherto have condemned them out of my blessed inexperience but now their simple homage gave us comfort. Constantly I scourged myself with thoughts of what I might have done to improve her lot. Amongst her things I had found a little handkerchief on which she had painstakingly embroided her initial – J. If only I had known, I would have bought her a dozen initialled handkies. I clutched it during her funeral and bedewed it with my tears. I would never part with it.

Dad, still inconsolable, went back with Hilda. When we fetched him home he stayed with us, though he would not give up the old house and visited it daily with mournful nostalgia. Absentmindedly I still accumulated bits of gossip, William pears and bronze chrysanthemums, before remembering Mother was no longer here to give them to.

Father was the first of the bra burners. When he saw three of varying sizes blowing on the line he was outraged and took the law into his own hands. He would never have credited me with such behaviour, he said, for they were only designed to titillate the opposite sex. In vain I denied this, and explained to him they were worn for comfort. 'Your Mother never wore one in her life!' he cried. 'And look what a lovely woman she was.' Argument was useless. I set up a line in the bedroom and thereafter our smalls were dried there.

One day I came home from work to find Judith toasting tea-cakes and they smelled heavenly. She took me in at a glance, pushed me into a chair, pulled off my shoes and plonked the plate of tea-cake on my lap. 'Eat it!' she commanded, 'O I forgot – you'll want to scrub your hands.' She took the plate off me again, pushed a great hunk into my mouth and another in her own. 'I'll do some more,' she said thickly through her own hunk and impaling another split tea-cake on the toasting fork commenced to do so. 'I missed my lunch at school today and now I'm so hungry,' she went on. 'Why did you miss your lunch?' I asked. 'I was sick and I had the most terrible headache. Mom I've never been so ill in my life, they put me in sick bay, but not to worry, I'm fine now and famished. 'I looked at her anxiously. She'd never had anything worse than chicken pox, I did hope she wasn't going to start with migraines.

* * *

When he was ten years old Bo'sun had a stroke. I saw it happen before my very eyes. We had just come in. He was stretched on the hearthrug before the fire and I was drinking tea when he went to get up and couldn't. I knew immediately what had happened, and when he looked at me with his beautiful eyes, confident that whatever was wrong I would be able to put right, and his long neck twisted at an abnormal angle, I went to pieces and falling on my knees beside him I wept uncontrollably.

I didn't call the vet, for the thought of having him put down was too unbearable. But when he came home GL refuted that; he too loved Bo'sun but couldn't see him suffer. The vet, however, had no such intentions. 'He may improve in a few days,' he said, and sure enough within a week Bo'sun had full use of his limbs again and in no time was racing round the common with his usual verve. He never had a recurrence and I used to take him to visit my discouraged stroke cases to give them fresh impetus. Four years later he began to weary; old age and a failing heart, diagnosed the vet, and one evening when he fell asleep on my lap, for he dearly loved to be nursed, he never woke again. I never saw a more peaceful death.

His passing was a great loss to us all but to poor Bandy, the kitten I had rescued from old Eli's, it was traumatic. For days he lay in the basket they had shared refusing food and moaning pitiably, and for a long time we feared we would lose him too.

The grief of losing a beloved pet that we have outlived can only be assuaged by the thought of how much worse it would have been for them had they outlived us.

It is the dear familiar things that we most cherish. When Judith was very young Peg had given her a rag doll; it was dressed as a colourful swashbuckling pirate and fired Judith's imagination. During the day he lay on top of her bed and during the night shared it with her, and she always insisted on taking him on holiday, even on a school holiday to Austria with her luggage packed to capacity.

Another of her treasures was a little blue chest of drawers given to her by Auntie Lilian. It was just big enough to accommodate dolls' clothes but in it she kept her small secret treasures and it was a matter of honour that no one violated it.

Judith had now left school and was attending a college of further education but she continued with her dancing and modelling and planned to make it her profession when her education was complete. Both girls had a legacy from Mother and she planned to use hers for further training. We had been told that she had great stage presence and her mind was set upon theatricals.

My husband meanwhile had settled happily in his job as an ambulance man and was soon to become a station officer.

Without coercion he had lost his taste for a tipple, and on the most social occasion he would seldom take more than one, having seen the results of drunken driving at first hand.

Not that the drunk had to be a driver. One night he was called out by some people who said a man had collapsed on their driveway. He found the man lying helpless. He had trespassed on the driveway to answer the call of nature but was so drunk that afterwards when putting his trousers back on he had put both legs down the same trouser leg and rendered himself helpless!

A more rewarding service was delivering babies in the ambulance, and he became very adept at this.

Ivan who had been working on a farm a few miles away now obtained a more promising job in Shrewsbury, Shropshire, so he and Elizabeth decided to marry and put a deposit on a little house near the river.

The bridesmaids' dresses were blue with pink floral wreaths for their hair and pink posies for bouquets. Elizabeth's dress was white satin, simply cut with a fitted bodice and the hint of a bustle and train to the full skirt.

'And what are you wearing?' asked Rose with whom I had gone to Sunday School and whose old mother I was now attending.

'Green,' I answered vaguely.

'Oh no!' she cried. 'Please don't wear green!'

'Why ever not?'

'Black follows green,' she quoted distressfully.

'Now who've we got who could die?' I laughed facetiously and remembering Father immediately regretted it.

I wore the green with a little floral hat and Gun-layer was resplendent in morning suit and gray topper (courtesy of Moss Bros.).

On the morning of the great day Elizabeth and Judith had gone for a last-minute hair do. The wedding was at two o'clock and at one they still hadn't returned. Since we had no idea which hairdresser they had gone to I got out the car and scoured the area. When I found them Judith was still under the drier.

I bundled them both into the car and home in time to get them into their glad-rags. Everyone but GL had left for the church. When they were finally launched I made frantic adjustments to myself before skedaddling in our own car by a different route. They arrived much later; the wedding car in taking a short cut had got held up for twenty minutes at the railway crossing. Poor Gun-layer with his obsession for punctuality!

It was a beautiful wedding. My new son-in-law, also in morning suit, made an elegant groom, until he knelt at the altar exposing '39/6' in white chalk on the soles of his shoes!

I stifled my laughter instead of shedding the traditional tears as mother of the bride.

*   *   *

The day after the wedding Judith had another of her sick headaches.

'It's the reaction,' they all said. 'She's upset at losing her sister.'

'But I haven't lost a sister,' quipped Judith between bouts of vomiting. 'I've only gained a telephone.'

Despite the enforced gaiety, put on for the benefit of visitors, I could see that she was feeling very ill and fear gnawed at my vitals. The blinding headache, as though induced by pressure from within, the violent retching which appeared to have no relation to food.

I knew now who we had who could die. In a few days she was herself again and then after a period of false quiet the malaise struck once more.

'Adolescence,' said the medicos. 'Typical of migraine.' Adding kindly, 'Nurses all worry unnecessarily about their children, imagine things that aren't there.'

Unconvinced I made an appointment to see the best eye specialist in the area and confided my fears in him. If they were justified his investigations could reveal the worst. He found nothing abnormal but this did not reassure me and I lived alone with my fear, taking it out in the lonely hours of the night to examine it with deep foreboding. Sometimes in the darkness I would hear the sound of retching and, creeping into her room, find her clutching her poor head with little animal moans, trying not to disturb the rest of the household.

Once more and privately I arranged for her to see a well-known specialist. Reluctantly she accompanied me to Edgebaston, the Harley Street of the Midlands, and again submitted to rigorous examination. It was one of her good days and there was a light-hearted rapport between her and the great man, as though it was an amusing exercise performed to humour a slightly dotty Mum. He could find nothing wrong with her: over-slim perhaps but she was small-boned and not built to carry weight. I should feel proud of so attractive a daughter. They parted most amicably, beaming indulgently upon the dotty Mum.

The next day she was struck down again. The attack was more severe and of longer duration. By now everyone but myself was convinced that her mysterious malady was migraine. Had I not always suffered from them? And were they not familial? Between attacks she was her usual bright self, performing for charities, modelling with Anne, her appetite unimpaired – except when terror struck.

During severe attacks pethidine was permissable. The first time I gave her the injection the result was dramatic: in a very short while the attack was over.

'Oh Mom,' she said, 'I shan't ever worry again if you can give me that, it's magic!' But I knew the magic wouldn't last when she had become accustomed to it.

Once a week, on my day off, we visited Elizabeth in Shrewsbury and we always made it an occasion. Ivan had worked so hard to improve their little house and the garden which sloped right down to the river. Elizabeth had become quite domesticated and was now expecting a baby; the thought of becoming a grandmother was the one thing that sustained me. Judith too was delighted with the prospect of being an aunt; it gave her a new interest. If ever a family needed new life, ours did.

Before Elizabeth's baby was due she was rushed to hospital with very high blood pressure and given an induction to induce labour by artificial means. Days passed without results. When phoned the hospital were non-committal and we were beside ourselves with anxiety.

Saturday came and I visited all of my patients to tell them that I was off-duty for a few days but a relief nurse would attend them.

While I was dressing Mrs Tibbs's poor legs and before I could tell her, she said, 'Yo' needn't worry about yer daughter any more, er's 'ad a bouncing boy.'

'You're an old witch!' I teased. 'How could you know?'

'That's a bloody tarradiddle!' she cried, grossly affronted. 'An' I do know because I've 'ad the bally ache all night.'

As soon as I could escape I hurried home and phoned the hospital again. I was told to hold the line and held it so long I feared the worst. When an anonymous voice told me that she had just had a son the relief was such that speech was impossible and Judith, waiting anxiously beside me, cried, 'She's dead, isn't she? She's dead – tell me!' and she shook me fiercely as though to dislodge the words and when she did so we embraced each other and wept for joy.

Despite so rough a passage the child survived. Ivan, standing in the bus queue en route for his first visit, could contain himself no longer. 'I've got a son! I've got a son!' he announced to the astonished crowd and stirred by his exaltation they surrounded him with handshakes and congratulations.

I didn't take my days off; only husbands could visit anyway. Instead I saved them until Elizabeth and her baby were allowed home and then we were able to collect them with the car. Waiting for her in the entrance hall I saw my grandson for the first time. He was in his father's arms – lint white hair and a skin like alabaster (not an Albino surely!). I peered at him anxiously to see if his eyes were pink but when he opened them they were a beautiful blue. His father was staring at him besotted, his lips all of a twitch. In this trance-like state I drove them home with the utmost care.

To become an aunt was the best gift Judith could have had at that time; it helped to take her mind off her own troubles. His parents decided to name their son Andrew George.

'Do you think they'll ask me to be his godmother?' asked Judith. 'If they do, and I don't have any children of my own, I would like him to have my money.' I looked at her suspiciously and made no comment but stored her words at the back of my mind. She took great note of Mother's legacy and the interest was totting up encouragingly. They did ask her, and she took her duties very seriously.

*   *   *

We had been dogless since Bo'sun's death, mainly because we felt that none could replace him. Now I wondered if a dog would be a help to Judith, who was so very fond of animals. If so, it must be small, easy for her to handle, biddable and intelligent, and nothing filled these requirements more than my old love the griffon. Griffons were not easily come by but we heard of a kennels at Penkridge with a litter for sale and on my next day off we went to see them.

The little mother curled protectively around her suckling brood and eyed us anxiously. She was not belligerent for her life was spent as a brood bitch and she knew from long experience that strangers would come and take her babies away, but not unweaned. These were her halcyon days, filled with loving and giving and deep fulfilment.

Deftly, with experienced hands, the owner winkled her treasures from their mother's dugs. The first four were dogs and equally adorable but the fifth she left in the nest for she was the only bitch of the litter and was being retained for future breeding.

Immediately I knew it was a bitch we must have for then we could breed from her ourselves, eventually keeping one of her daughters to perpetuate the line. I saw a long vista of little bitches each bequeathing us a fruitful female so that we would never again suffer the complete traumatic loss which had followed Bo'sun's demise. Not only that, it would give Judith a new interest and a lucrative hobby.

I hardened myself to the charms of the dog pups; we must look elsewhere. But the owner relented; we had found favour in her eyes and most griffon breeders desire a good home for their pups, selecting buyers discriminately.

It was left to Judith to care for her, house-train her and of course choose her name. Her registered name was Suval Revelry, and as though she knew she stubbornly refused to answer to any name but Su though inevitably the derivative Susie was finally accepted. We wondered how Bandy would regard the intrusion and made much of him because if it, but he chose to ignore her and stayed aloof and out of reach.

*   *   *

One day while on my round I met our own doctor who had not seen Judith for some time, though he had received the reassuring reports from the consultants to whom I had taken her. When he asked how she was I replied that she was 'falling apart in front of me' and hurried away while I still had control of myself.

That evening he phoned. 'I made an excuse to call today,' he said. 'Judith answered the door to me. I do agree there is something very wrong with her.' The dread words only filled me with relief; at last someone else recognized it too. He went on to say he was sending her to hospital for investigation.

Poor Judy! She was so reluctant to go. The hospital was a teaching school of very high repute so I told her what I feared: that she had a brain tumour, for I knew it would be discussed before her, as indeed it was. I added that most were benign and when removed gave no further trouble.

She was in a women's ward for she was now fifteen and I was told how helpful she was with her fellow patients. She was in apparent good health and all the investigations showed nothing abnormal. Then one day I found her in a state of excitement.

'Mom!' she said importantly. 'When one of the students was looking in my eyes today with her gadget she found I'd had five haemorrhages on my fungus!'

'You mean fundus.' I laughed, but it was a hollow laugh and my heart had taken a sickening plunge for this was it.

From then things were set in motion with alarming speed.

204

An eminent brain surgeon from London was to carry out an investigation. It was one only performed when all else has failed, the pain afterwards would be very severe due to pressure and – of course – the head must be shaved.

Judith was very distressed when next I saw her. 'They're going to do such terrible things Mom. Please don't let them,' she pleaded, and I wished they had spared her the unnecessary details.

She was to have her head shaved that afternoon in front of an audience of nurses, who must of course be taught how to do it.

The next day the investigation took place. Late that night we had a phone call from the hospital. They wished us to know the results: a large mass had been revealed at the base of her skull and the surgeon would be operating at nine o'clock the following morning.

My husband and I spent a sleepless night and set off early in order to see her before she went to the theatre. It was a long drive to the hospital. She was very brave and full of hope and I was allowed to accompany her to the theatre doors. There was a large gathering of medical students excitedly waiting to see the great man perform.

Although the time seemed endless before she was returned to the ward yet still it was too soon, for had the operation been successful it would have taken much longer. We sat beside her bed waiting for her to regain consciousness and dreading the moment when she would, but when she did she was mercifully sedated. We had not eaten all day and I persuaded my husband to go out for a meal. While he was away a message came from the surgeon who wished to see us. He was a kindly man and it was obvious that he found it very difficult to say what he had to.

'I think,' I said gently, 'that I am prepared for the worst.' But I was not prepared for the worst; one of the things he had to tell me was that before long Judith would almost certainly go blind.

I was thankful that GL was not there to hear the dread news and resolved not to tell him, or indeed anyone.

The senior consultant under whom Judith had been admitted was ironically the one to whom I had taken her in Edgebaston. He was most sympathetic and explained that the tumour was in the dark areas of the brain and could not have been detected without the drastic investigation which, because of the risk, was not carried out except in extreme circumstances. A veil was diplomatically drawn over the eye specialist who should surely have seen what a mere student discovered. Dog doesn't eat dog. Not that it would have made much difference: the tumour must have been growing all her life but was not made manifest until the size caused pressure. Since then the great advance in brain surgery and the detection of abnormalities could probably have saved her.

Before the shaving I had asked for a lock of her hair. Wigs were not then the vogue but I took it to a salon and asked if they could obtain a matching one in real hair. They were most helpful and on her first outing after coming home we went to find they had quite a selection of adjustable pieces for her to try on. She chose a simple style, short but with a fringe such as she normally wore; the transformation was quite wonderful and gave her ego a terrific boost. The assistants who could not have been kinder were delighted with their success.

Diplomatically they concealed their horror on seeing the site of the operation on the back of her head – a deep perpendicular scar from the crown to the neck line was bisected by a horizontal one from ear to ear.

It was a perfect replica of the cross.

*   *   *

With her natural resilience Judith became active again. Family and friends from far and wide rallied, and every day there was a wealth of post.

My colleagues too had rallied. When Judith was in hospital I had worked until three every day and then been free to visit her; now I decided to give in my notice to be with her full time, but the MOH refused it, and he was adamant.

206

Later, he hinted, I would need my job to keep on an even keel. Later was something I didn't want to think about. Judith was so much better, and the principal of her college had suggested that she might like to return and if she became unwell she could go into sick bay until I could collect her. That clinched it; she went happily back to college and I less happily to work.

Every moment she was out of my sight I feared for her. The remission was an unexpected bonus and I mustn't spoil it by being over-protective, but I was haunted by her threatened blindness.

She brought friends home from college. Four of them tended to go around together, and they were protective towards her and knew that if she was unwell they must phone for me. Then the gang inevitably split up into two couples so here I was with a vulnerable male on my hands, made more difficult because Rob, Judith's partner, was so likeable and so obviously devoted to her.

Although she never went out without her hairpiece her own hair was beginning to grow again, thick dark and like plush. Elizabeth said she looked like a little Italian boy and Rob agreed. He washed and massaged her scalp with loving care and there was nothing she found more soothing. One day they came from college convulsed with laughter; during a scrimmage in the cloakroom a boy had pulled Judith's hair and it had come off in his hand. 'Their faces!' she cried. 'Mom, it was the funniest thing I've ever seen!'

Although she never went to dancing school again she still loved to dance and I knew that escorted by Rob she was as safe as could be. Once when with GL and myself I was amazed at her agility and the fact that despite such brain damage her sense of balance was unimpaired. The new dances were so vigorous and uninhibited but she never lacked partners and once the floor automatically cleared as she and her companion demonstrated an incredible jive.

At college, too, despite her long absence she held her own, taking exams with her fellow students and gaining honours in maths and physics. I still have her last report in which she is described as being 'exceptional'.

Sadly I woke one night to the familiar sounds of violent retching. Her symptoms had returned doublefold and the pethidine no longer took effect.

'I'm not cured really, am I Mom? It's starting all over again.'

From then she deteriorated, several good days followed by several bad. We moved into the bedroom with twin beds so that I was always near and she could put out a hand in the night to touch me and know that she was not alone.

She improved sufficiently to go with Rob to the St Valentine's dance. I took them in the car as I always did but promised to collect them early before she tired. When I arrived Rob came to me on the car park. 'She's having a whale of a time,' he said.

'Then don't tell her I'm here, stay until the end if you like. I don't mind how long I wait.'

These were precious days – and the last dance of all.

Now the fear of her eventual blindness was always with me. Ungodly though I was, I prayed nightly to whoever might be up there to take this last cup from her. 'Let it be me,' I beseeched, 'and I will never complain.'

When Susie had her first birthday Judy and Rob gave a party for her. They did the catering and savouries were the order of the day, though they did produce a birthday cake with a tree in the centre in lieu of a candle.

When Susie came on heat for the second time Judith and Rob went to the Championship Show at Birmingham and by dint of much know-how, garnered from the griffon group, chose a mate for her. When I took her to be served she was not enamoured with him but as always she was anxious to please. The ensuing pregnancy left her morose, moody and beset with bile, and she carried the pups like a sack of potatoes.

Poor little Susie! I promised her she would never have to repeat the experience; it was only for Judith's sake she was doing it now. When she pupped she would be happy, I thought, but she wasn't; she had no maternal instinct at all.

Patiently Judith and Rob held the pups to her to let them suckle, which they did voraciously, but she gave them no encouragement and afterwards they bumbled about in their box mewling piteously and rejected. It took old Bandy to size up the situation; he went hunting and returned with a fat freshly killed mouse which he dropped in the box with them.

'Why,' cried Father, 'they're hungry and Bandy knows it!'

And he was right. Their greedy suckling had got them nowhere, for Susie had no milk. The mother instinct is to feed, but what can she do if she has nothing to offer them?

Hastily I mixed baby food and we set to feeding them with an eye dropper. They were ravenous and took it eagerly. Later I added egg-yolk, honey and crushed calcium to the milk and we used premature baby bottles. We enlisted the help of the vet, but despite his treatment Susie never produced any milk. She watched her progeny's progress and kept her distance.

Judith was not now well enough to attend college but she had a full time job caring for the pups, for as well as being fed they had to be kept scrupulously clean and after each feed their tummies had to be gently massaged, which is what the mother normally does with her tongue to encourage their natural functions. I bought a little china pot and they performed like well-trained babies. Everyone who came found themselves lumbered with a bottle and a pup. It became quite a cult among the collegians and they forgot it was Judith they had come to see.

Gun-layer had fitted a heater for the pups and Judith added her old teddy bear. They snuggled up to his furry body and he became their surrogate mum with a ticking clock bandaged to his tum to simulate her heartbeats. They had now taken over the lounge and the whole place flowed with milk and honey, but all four were dogs and so my vista of little bitches never materialized.

When Judith registered them with the Kennel Club she longed to have a prefix. It is usually the name of the kennel but the names are never duplicated and it was difficult to think up one that had not already been used. Amongst her friends she had always been known as Jot and she reckoned that by incorporating it she could surmount the problem and Susie's sons became Jot's Jiminy, Jot's Jester, Jot's Junior, and Jot's Jingo. When she received their certificates bearing 'Breeder – Judith Cotterill' she felt very important.

We would never have become successful breeders for we gave two of the pups away and sold the others for a minimum to what we felt sure were ideal homes, but they had served their purpose and helped their ill-fated young breeder through an ever darkening patch.

*   *   *

She was very brave but was now getting circulatory complications. At times she had great pain in her feet and her hitherto supple limbs were becoming stiff and immobile but she sought only not to distress us.

I was now working part-time and my patients and colleagues could not have been more helpful and considerate. Judith was spending the mornings in bed, usually joined by Susie and Bandy, for they wanted to be with her all the time and lay on a travelling rug on the bed.

Once after a very severe attack she was unconscious for three days. Elizabeth came and we sat at her bedside hoping that she would never come round again, but she did. Quite suddenly she opened her eyes and said slowly and clearly, 'Something's happened to Peter Sellars.'

Elizabeth and I stared at each other. Whatever had made her say that? We'd never heard her mention him before. But Judith was on to more mundane matters – she was hungry and she would like a drink, please.

She was better than she had been for weeks and chattered brightly, but she didn't mention Peter Sellars again.

It was obvious that she was not going to leave us for awhile and Elizabeth had her own commitments, so GL got out the car and drove her home. Later that night she phoned.

'Mom, did you hear the news?'

'Yes dear.'

'About Peter Sellars?'

'Yes dear.' They had said that Peter Sellars, who was in America, had suffered a heart attack. Despite attempted resuscitation he had died, but a young medico had insisted on continuing and amazingly he recovered. We discussed the phenomenon, then and many times since, but are no nearer an explanation.

Sunday, May the 10th, was Judith's seventeenth birthday. Although she was taking nothing by mouth she'd had a night of continuous retching. Morphine injections which eased the pain in her head aggravated the vomiting; now she was pitifully weak and exhausted. Through the open window drifted the strains of the morning service on a nearby radio.

> Let us with a gladsome mind
> Praise the Lord for he is kind.

We knew better: the Lord is not always kind.

At last she fell into uneasy slumber. How different this day should have been. I remembered Elizabeth's seventeenth birthday and the little rhyme we had composed for her – and my promise.

'Promise, Mom, promise you'll write one to me when I'm seventeen.'

Sitting at her bedside I wrote it.

> Beloved child, each tortured breath
> Beseeches me to speed your death.
> Forgive me, though I hear your call
> I lack the grace to end it all.
> Outside the spring has come again
> The garden's fresh with falling rain,
> Was it the rain, or gentle dew
> That brought this evil thing to you?
> O scientist! Misguided sage!
> Your fall-out of this nuclear age

211

Must surely be the foulest crime
Committed since the dawn of time.
My child is dying, but the spell
Lies deep within your child as well.
I pray you, do not weep for me,
The bell is tolling too for thee.

I hid it away. Although she would never read it, it belonged to Judith.

*   *   *

Throughout the day there was a constant stream of callers bearing gifts. She insisted on seeing them all and thanking them personally. I labelled each offering; later they would be returned with gratitude for the pleasure they had given her.

On Thursday I asked GL to fetch Elizabeth. They had been for Judy's birthday but time was getting short and even in these last hours she took a gentle delight in seeing Andrew.

That night as I prepared for bed Judith said, 'Mom, why don't you put the light on? It's getting so dark.'

'I can manage dear,' I replied, and didn't tell her the light was on. As usual I pushed my bed alongside hers and lay on the top in my dressing gown. We held hands and with a soft pressure on mine she said, 'You've been a lovely Mum.' Shortly after she drifted into a last sleep and a blessed unconsciousness.

During the night Cheyne Stokes breathing took over and as day broke I crept into my husband's room and switched off his alarm clock. He stirred and looked inquiringly. 'You won't be going to work,' I said. 'Judith will die today.'

Later in the morning the rhythm of her breathing changed. Quickly I knelt by the bed and slipped my hand into hers. Her fingers curled automatically round mine like those of a sleeping babe and she suddenly became so very young and vulnerable, like a creature emerging from a chrysalis into a new life. It was a beauty so fleeting I held my

212

breath in wonder – and in the room there was no breathing at all.

Outside in the garden Andrew shouted aloud and the little dog barked. I looked at the clock. It was 10.30 a.m., 15 May, Elizabeth's twenty-third birthday. Just then she came into the room and saw that it was over. The dying need only a hand to hold and a quiet in which to make their departure.

One hour later I laid her out and dressed her in the frilly primrose pyjamas she loved. I kissed those dancing feet, now discoloured and swollen by pain, and stilled forever. Her features were set in a doll-like mask and all the wonder was gone.

The news spread. All day people called to offer condolences. Poor Rob came to be comforted and stayed to share our grief, as did Ivan; neither had ever believed she would really die.

Elizabeth had lost not only her sister, she had lost her birthday. Never again would she accept a card or gift; the decision was her own. It was Whitsun weekend and so the funeral must wait until Tuesday, but the coffin was brought and Judy was put into it. When the undertakers had gone and I saw her in an ugly beige-coloured shroud I was affronted. She whose taste in clothes was so impeccable. Incongruously I thought she wouldn't have been seen dead in it – neither should she. I snatched off the offending garment, not difficult for it was in three separate pieces, so made to be put on without disturbing the cadaver. I stuffed them under the coverings and she lay again in her pretty primrose.

Sacrilegiously the sun shone when funeral time came. We put on our mourning and followed the coffin into the sunlight. She wasn't alone in it; at the last moment I had slipped in her pirate doll, Rob's loving Christmas, birthday and Valentine cards and my poem. The centuries haven't changed us; even prehistoric man had left the dead their little treasures for the long journey. As the simple cortège moved off I clutched Mother's handkerchief and didn't bother to think of Christ; it didn't matter any more, but no tears would come.

On the streets groups of people stood weeping and once more I was filled with gratitude. They were our friends and neighbours, people who had loved her too, offering comfort in the only way they could. Far up Edward Road I glimpsed my dear Peg, seeking to make her small self look even smaller, but when we turned the corner, out of sight, her spirit came forward and comforted me all the way.

The driver chose a quiet unfrequented route to Gornal crematorium but it was one we had travelled before, in the opposite direction, seventeen years ago to the hour and the day when we had brought home 'a sister for Elizabeth'.

We made the return journey with a sense of indescribable loss and a feeling of having received a mortal wound, a hurt too fearful to bear investigation but to be kept hidden from view lest the sight of it turn the mind.

Elizabeth and Ivan were having Judith's name inscribed in the Book of Memory at the crematorium and we were donating rose trees for their garden, but how I wished we could have afforded some worthwhile memorial to her; she warranted that.

At home Joyce was awaiting us, a buffet meal prepared for the proprieties must be observed. Her hosting of it gave me leave to escape to the sanctuary of our bedroom again. The imprint of the coffin lay a mute reminder upon the sheet; absentmindedly I smoothed it out and took down her little chest of drawers. Sometime I must go through this, disposing of its small secrets, and now was as good a time as any. But she had been there before me. Now it contained only an envelope, the word Mother scrawled across it like a spoken word.

It contained no last farewell letter – only a tiny newspaper cutting. The small print was blurred with unshed tears but when I had composed myself I read:

When some great sorrow, like a mighty river
Flows through your life with peace-destroying power

214

And dearest things are swept from sight for ever,
Say to yourself each trying hour
This too will pass away.

I sat for a while with it in my hand, but I didn't want it to 'Pass away'. I wanted to remember her always. Then a thought, like a wind-borne seed, settled and took root. I had always wanted to write, now I would begin and any remuneration should go to her charities – that would be her memorial.

Filled with a creative urge I seized a pencil and began scribbling on the back of the envelope.

Perhaps, after all, the wound would heal.

A Glossary of
— Blackcountry Terms —
For the Uninitiated

Ack Dum At once
Ahviers Share
Aive Heave
Aiven day Easter Monday
Aks Ask
Appund Apron
Backen To keep back
Backerapper Explosive firework
Bally Belly
Bawk Confuse
Belluck Bellow
Beesum Pert young woman
Bibble Pebble
Blether yed A fool
Blobmouth Indiscreet Person
Bobowler Large moth
Boffle To hinder
Bonk Small hill (*Climbin' up the bonk o' forty* – Near middle age)
Bost Burst
Broo'us Brewhouse
Bunny fire Bonfire
Bunt Jostle
Buz Bus
Cack Excreta
Cag mag Gossip
Camplin Gossiping
Caggy Left Handed
Caw Cannot
Chicklings Pig's intestines

216

Chimdy Chimney
Chops Mouth
Chunter To grumble
Clammed Hungry
Coddin' Joking
Codge modge Rough work
Cost Could you? (*Thee cosn't* – You can't)
Croodle Huddle together
Cut Canal
Dishle o' tay Cup of tea
Don 'and Expert
Dunny Hard of hearing
Dunderhead A Dolt or numbskull
Fittle Food, Victuals
Fizog Face, Visage
Flen Flea
Fode Fold, Yard (Back Yard)
Frowsty Dishevelled
Ganzy Under vest
Gammitin' Playing the fool
Gammy Lame
Gawby Simpleton
Groaty Dick Groats and meat stewed together
Gawp To stare open mouthed
Guffaw Coarse laughter
Guttle Gobble
Ines Woman
Ivver ovver Hesitate
Keffle A lumbering fellow
Kench To sprain
Lampin' Thrashing
Loff Laugh
Munch Ill treat
Mumchance Doleful, Dejected
Miskin Privy
"Marry the miskin fer the muck an' git pizened wi' the stink on it" To
    marry for money and live to regret it
Naither Neither
Nairun None
Nash Weakling
Nerker Mischievous (Child)
Nineter A Tarter, A terrible fellow

217

Node Knew
Ockerd Awkward
Odge up Move up
Pail Beat
Pither Potter about
Potch To forestall or get the better of
Plonk Put down
Randy Big-mouthed
Rantan Violent
Racket Din or clamour
Ranter Primitive Methodist
Riffy Unclean, Crumby
Rigmarole Long unintelligible story
Rorty Satisfactory
Saided Sated, Glutted
Sawny Simple
Skrobble A tangle
Snape Snub
Splod Flat-footed
Strumpet Prostitute
Swopson Large, Heavy
Tank Sharp blow
Tarradiddle A fib or lie
Tater Potato
Togs Clothes
Traipse To wander about aimlessly
Tranklements Paraphernalia, Miscellaneous belongings
Tunkey Fat pig
Two double Doubled up with pain
Wairter Water
Werrit Worry
Wamble Nausea
Whigmaleerie A trinket or gewgaw
Whopper Anything large, A monstrous lie
Wonkey Shakey, Unsteady
Wull Whole
Wum Home
Xammer To complain peevishly
Yuck Itch
Oscillans Plumbi Swinging the lead (Latin)